SUPERSTARS OF GOLF

By NICK SEITZ

Swing Studies by BOB TOSKI

A Golf Digest Book

Photo Credits

Wilton Abel 11; Roy Attaway 79; Chuck Brenkus 126-129; Charlie Buchanan 8; Chan Bush 75, 100; Steve Craig/Black Star 52, 53; Courtesy Walt Disney Productions 84; Durst-Ireland Photography 18, 19; Bob East 68, 69; Frank Gardner 120, 155; Courtesy Golden Bear Enterprises 142, 143, 144, 145; Golf Digest photos 20-23, 38-41, 54-57, 146-149, 164-167; Will Hertzberg 7, 47, 63, 113, 130, 135, 151, 160; Leonard Kamsler 70-73, 90-93, 108-111, 182-185; Bill Knight 36, 37; Courtesy William Kosta & Associates 45; E. D. Lacey 117; Courtesy Miami-Metro Dept. of Tourism 17, 181 (upper); Ryan Miller 30; Bill Mount 87; Lester Nehamkin 25, 29, 33, 34, 58, 95, 98; David Oshin 103, 168, 175; Mel Page 115, 123; Courtesy Arnold Palmer 86, 88, 89; Courtesy Gary Player 162 (lower); Bill Romero 12; Tony Rose 124, 125; Peter Runyon 138; Wayne Sassano 104; Jack Scagnetti 42; Dick Severino 80, 81; Warren Skipper 27; John Titchen 136; Courtesy UMI 106 (upper), 107 (lower); UPI 48, 76, 106 (lower), 132, 133, 153, 154, 156, 171, 179; Isobel Van Der Spuy 162 (upper), 163 (lower); Courtesy Tom Weiskopf 180, 181 (lower); Wide World Photos 69 (center right)

Published by
Golf Digest, Inc.
A New York Times Company
495 Westport Avenue
Norwalk, Connecticut 06856

Trade book distribution
by Simon and Schuster
A Division of Gulf & Western Corporation
New York, New York 10020

First Printing
ISBN: 0-914178-13-X
Library of Congress: 77-92910
Manufactured in the United States of America

CONTENTS

to my parents, who love the game

Acknowledgements

The preparation of this book was made immeasurably easier and more fun by the ongoing assistance of the staff of *Golf Digest* magazine, particularly Charlene Cruson, coordinator of the books department, and Laura Duggan, art director of books. Also Larry Dennis, Ross Goodner, Sue Irvine, Lois Jamieson, Lois Hains, Patrick Leahy, Marven Moss, Dwayne Netland, Pat Richards, Jay Simon and Jerry Tarde. They all contributed substantially and unstintingly to the research and editing processes, and their efforts are appreciated.

N.S.

INTRODUCTION

What's Arnold Palmer *really* like? As a golf writer, I've been asked that question approximately 86,332 times in 25 states and on two ships at sea.

Arnold Palmer is having an affair with Laura Baugh, he prefers tennis to golf, and he eats chopped green lizards for breakfast.

Actually, none of that is true, so far as I know, but I've always wanted to give it for an answer, just for fun. What Arnold is truly like, on and off the course, I have tried to convey in one of the 10 chapters of this book. The other nine chapters are devoted to the other nine modern superstars.

Who qualifies as a superstar? The list is certainly open to argument—I have argued with myself about it at great length. All of the players I chose have won one or more of the four major professional tournaments and, with one exception, more than a million dollars in prize money. The exception is young Tom Watson, who had won "only" $838,962 through 1977, and if you would care to bet that he will not reach the million-dollar level in our lifetime (he may well have reached it by the time you read this), I know where you can find all the action you can transact.

Statistics alone do not make a superstar, however. There also is the transcending quality of charisma — a personal magnetism that captivates the fans and the media. These 10 players have it.

To established stars like Dave Stockton, Ben Crenshaw, Hubert Green and Jerry Pate, whom I did not include, I can only say that leaving you out for lack of space may have been the hardest the job.

The book was conceived as a simple enough assignment. I was to update profiles I had written for *Golf Digest* and pick a selection of tournament photographs from the magazine's files. But the project grew like Topsy. It was necessary to interview most of the players again. And new concepts kept presenting themselves. Why not a photographic essay on each player at home with his family and pursuing his off-course interests, to show the sides of him the public never sees?

And wouldn't the average golfer relish a chance to learn from the swings of these great players? And wouldn't Bob Toski, the superstar of teaching, be the natural choice to analyze sequence photos of those swings and relate them to us weekenders, pointing out what we should copy and what we should avoid to play better?

Now it was a three-dimensional book: an inquiring profile about each superstar and his philosophy of the game, an off-course photo essay, a relevant swing study by Toski. Now it was a revealingly rounded look at 10 men who play the most challenging game on earth better than anyone else and who, for all that they have in common, are compellingly strong individualists, dramatically different one from another.

What are they *really* like? This book will show and tell you.

—Nick Seitz
January, 1978

LEE TREVINO

Ever since he came from some-where south of nowhere to finish fifth in the 1967 U.S. Open at Baltusrol, Lee Trevino has led the league in laughs.

I still like the zinger he put on a middle-aged woman who was ooh-ing and aahing over his routine warm-up shots on the practice range one day. Trevino finally spun around, glared at her with mock disgust and yelped, "What did you expect from a million-dollar winner, lady — ground balls?"

At the World Series of Golf one year, shortly before the last round, Trevino sashayed over to Dave Hill on the range and, knowing Hill had stayed late at the club the night before, chirped, "Baby, I found 14 beer bottles in there with your fingerprints on 'em. That must have been some party."

Once he was in England play-ing a match against Tony Jacklin, then the resident national resource. A solemn Jacklin said before the match he didn't want to talk that day, he wanted to concentrate on his game.

Said Trevino, "You don't have to talk. Just listen. I'll talk enough for both of us. If I keep my mouth shut for four hours out here I'll have bad breath."

I first came to know Lee Trevino in 1970 when we were in Argen-tina for the World Cup. I thought it would be a good opportunity to do a story about him. He had not won a major championship in 1970, but was on his way to a great statisti-cal year — he ultimately won the money title, the tour points race and the Vardon Trophy for low stroke average, the triple crown of pro golf. More importantly, for a game that in modern times is some-times about as lively as choir prac-tice, Trevino had emerged as a folk hero. A wise-cracking, happy-go-lucky fellow from inauspicious be-ginnings, he had returned to golf that most endearingly human ele-

ment, a sense of humor.

The Spanish-chattering Trevino figured to captivate Buenos Aires even more completely than he had captivated the staid British in flamboyant trips to England and Scotland. As defending World Cup individual champion he was sure to be in the spotlight. That is where he is at his best, both as player and as entertainer.

My means of entry to closer acquaintance with Lee was traumatic. At the World Cup course (the Jockey Club) with "Waxo" Green, a columnist from Nashville, I figured to wait until all the pros had begun their practice rounds, then play a round quietly, out of sight of the Argentine fans already flocking to the course. But the first two people we encountered were Trevino and Dave Stockton, his partner on the U.S. team. We were carrying our clubs, and Trevino said: "Come on and play with us —we'll check your action." My fellow writer, to my unending mystification, leaped at the chance, and the next thing I knew we were on the first tee, which just happened to be surrounded by eight trillion people.

Trevino hit first, 270 yards up the middle. Stockton hit next, 260 up the middle. I cannot translate what the gallery was saying as Waxo and I haltingly prepared to follow, but I am pretty sure it was Spanish for "Who in blazes are these clowns?" Waxo laced a respectable 220-yard shot out into the fairway. I addressed my ball through what seemed a heavy fog, and asked myself what ever possessed me to buy bell-bottomed golf slacks. Frantically, I smashed a 200-yarder that almost stayed out of the left rough. My relief at even making contact with the ball was immense, and my caddie looked at me quizzically when I sighed loudly.

There was light rough on the fairway for the first 200 yards or so of each hole, and because Trevino and Stockton insisted on playing from as far back as possible, Waxo and I were having a hard time hitting far enough to reach the fairway. The strain soon told. On the sixth tee, a narrow chute, I hit a dead pull, 800 miles an hour, on a trajectory never higher than three feet. About 75 yards out, it screamed past the right ear of an astonished lady sitting on a shooting stick. Before she had time to register her alarm, however, the ball crashed into a gallery rope stake—and whistled back past her left ear! At this, she tumbled off the shooting stick. She probably will never go to a golf course again.

After that, as I stepped up to each tee shot, Trevino hollered, "Fore everywhere!" He explained that he wouldn't kid me like this if he hadn't seen that I was a good sport, and a rapport of some sort was established between us.

Once I had collected myself during the round, I studied Trevino as he and Stockton strode along analyzing the course. He demonstrated his exceptional knack for regaling the crowd with a joke during a swing, more often than not delivering the punch line exactly at impact. This was the Trevino I had heard so much about—the garrulous madcap with loud red socks

and a pitcher of tequila nearby, the young hustler from the legendary muni courses of Texas, where everything is bigger than reality—cockily grateful for all the fame and fortune that had befallen him since, an unknown, he won the U.S. Open with a record-tying 275 at Rochester in 1968 and dubbed himself "Super Mexkin" or SuperMex for short. "Soon as I make me a little more money," he joked, "I'm gonna be a Spaniard instead of a Mexkin." Funny ole Lee, right?

From a distance, I had suspected that from inside this jocular, blithe, bubbly spirit an inherently serious character might be trying to emerge. Up close, that impression is verified. Away from the gallery, talking with Stockton in the fairway, Trevino acted thoroughly businesslike, pacing off a measurement from one landmark to another, testing the texture of the sand in a bunker, stressing aloud how much he wanted to defend his World Cup championship. I remembered Larry Ziegler saying, "You shouldn't let all that noise he makes fool you. He's as serious about his game as anyone else on the tour." I further had suspected that this seriousness extends beyond golf, having deep roots in a background marked as much by determined, self-taught struggling as by his celebrated proclivity for making people laugh.

Trevino said he would be happy to meet after the pro-am and talk about himself, and later at the hotel I sat with his wife Claudia and Bruce Devlin's wife Gloria in the dining room at tea time, the period late in the afternoon that helps kill the hours until dinner, never served until at least 11 p.m. Devlin's wife was saying how she flew on the same plane with Lee from the U.S. to Australia recently, and he had been a great help entertaining her children. "I can't believe that man," she said to Trevino's wife. "He talked non-stop the entire 14 hours."

"I can believe him," said Claudia Trevino, a pretty, slender blonde who frequently feuds with Lee, but fetchingly. "He gets up at 7 in the morning and starts chirping like that. I can't stand it. We don't speak till noon. It's just his nature. He likes to talk while he plays golf, because it relaxes him."

Mrs. Trevino added that her husband's loquaciousness too often is confused with unbounded gregariousness. "People think he parties every night. He does party a lot, especially if he's shot a bad round. But once a tournament has started he gets tired of all the attention. He orders most of his meals from room service. He came in steaming last night after the tournament dinner dragged on for three hours."

Trevino ambled up to the table, enthusing about the beautiful Argentine women, among the most stylish in the world. "Honey," he piped, "if I'da known what it was like down here, I'da left you at home."

"You're hopeless," she said.

Bantering back and forth, they got up and vanished into the elevator. Back in El Paso, where each has a hot new car, they drag-race each other on the country roads near their house.

The next day, after the pro-am (which I found a comparative breeze in the unspectacular company of the Rumanian team), I drove back to town with the Trevinos and at the hotel we ordered the excellent local beer in the bar. "I can remember when I was a kid with no money we used to pool our pennies and buy Tom Collins mix and pretend we were drunk," Lee said. "I love livin'. Why go to bed? I like to party because I missed a lot of nights when I couldn't afford parties. I get my five hours sleep."

But at the Westchester Classic one year, Trevino blew his first-round tee time and was disqualified. He said he overslept and denied the rumor he actually was in Atlantic City and never made it to bed. Said a successful veteran professional: "He could be one of the all-time greats, but if he's not careful he's going to burn out. There's the nightlife, plus he's playing 35 tournaments a year and running himself ragged with commercial activities on the side." Trevino himself, after the Westchester episode, said he was liable to become the only man ever to spend three years on tour and the rest in the nut house.

"I'm cuttin' back," Lee said firmly and animatedly. "I won the Open and I felt I had to play everywhere to help the sponsors. I just kept goin'. I didn't want to lay back for the big, expensive tournaments the way so many guys do. The little sponsors might be the big guys some day. And I like to play foreign events because my big ambition is to be an international champion. I may be from the

Marines and a driving range, but I taught myself how to play this game."

Lee can be uncommonly generous toward sponsors and toward just plain folks. He gave $10,000 of his purse from winning the 1968 Hawaiian Open to start a trust fund for the college education of the son of Ted Makalena, a Hawaiian pro and friend who had died two months earlier. One year he gave his $2,000 winnings at the World Cup to establish a scholarship fund for caddies in Singapore. If the gifts amounted to tax writeoffs, the sentiment was no less genuine, and he has been as quick to give his time as he has his money.

"I'm makin' two and three personal appearances a week even during tournaments, sometimes for myself and sometimes for charity, but I'm gonna slow down," he said. Maybe so, I said, but all notable modern precedents argued that he wouldn't. Once a superstar gets on the treadmill, he seldom jumps off. Although he frequently protests that he should and probably often wants to, he becomes locked in by snow-balling, long-term commitments. Trevino conceded that this is a major reason why so many young and relatively unknown players win. "It's not that the top players aren't as good as ever. It's that they don't have time to practice enough with all the other commitments."

The 1970 World Cup began and Trevino was jovial on the course. When the first three in his group Thursday drove far to the right, behind a clump of trees, he cracked:

"What's over there? A nudist colony?" He exclaimed in Spanish after long drives, and blew big pink bubbles with his bubblegum, and went through a funny impromptu bullfighting routine with a bee that bothered him as he tried to line up a putt. The big gallery loved it. "Too many pros come out here looking square-faced and forget that the crowd pays a lot of money to watch," he said later. "I'm lucky 'cause I was born to make people laugh. I enjoy makin' 'em laugh."

On the 18th, he made a remarkable recovery shot, close to the pin, and the crowd in the bleachers hollered its pleasure. Trevino's wife smiled. "He's such a big ham," she said fondly/sardonically. "I'm sure he birdies the 18th more than any other hole, because that's where most of the fans congregate."

As the World Cup progressed, however, Trevino's popularity waned. Local hero Roberto de Vicenzo moved into the individual lead and drew off a majority of the fans. Trevino putted badly on what were, by American standards, poor greens—thinly grassed and bumpy. Walking from a three-putt green to the next tee on Friday, he grumped loudly to his wife and me: "These greens are so bad the Dallas Cowboys wouldn't play on 'em. They ought to plow 'em up and plant 'em with potatoes." He said it in English, possibly assuming that the local gallery would not understand him, and possibly reckoning —rightly—that there were no Argentine reporters present. But someone in the gallery relayed a reasonably accurate translation of his remarks to a local newsman, and they were printed in the following morning's paper, along with some blistering editorial comment on Trevino's "lack of sportsmanship." Cup officials were just as dismayed. One said: "Bob Hope is the only man in the world who ought to try to be funny."

The final two days Trevino continued to miss putts and, rather than complain publicly about the greens, compounded his public relations troubles by avoiding the local press. It was the end of the year, he was suddenly tired and irritable, and all in all it was not a good week for him. "I just wanta get out a here without hurtin' myself," he said more than once, at a loss for fresh material. He took dinner in his room and boarded the first plane for the States.

Trevino's show must go on, but he was unhappily caught in the role of star entertainer and wasn't up to playing the part. Sometimes even Bob Hope has off nights. The serious side of Lee Trevino, the guy who worked day and night for a dozen or more years to become an overnight success, was there for all to see, and it's just as well that there weren't more people to see it.

The question in my mind after that week with Lee in 1970 was whether he could develop a sense of pace. His joviality would never desert him for long at a time—it was too solidly ingrained in his compulsive entertainer's nature. But the

Trevino, a solid putter, wants to feel that the heel of the putter is leading the toe into the ball. That way, he says, he'll avoid the common tendency to close the face.

13

other Lee Trevino—the serious Lee Trevino, just as real—would have to assert himself and serve as a better governor on the racing motor of his lighter side. I had hoped then he would make the adjustment and last another 20 years, because, Lord knows, this sport needs him.

As it turned out, the major crisis in Trevino's career came late in 1976 when he underwent lower-back surgery. In the interim he had won the U.S. Open again, beating Jack Nicklaus in a playoff at Merion in 1971, the year Lee also won the Canadian and British championships in a span of only five weeks. And he had won the British Open again in 1972 and the PGA Championship in 1974.

They operated on his back, but they didn't cut into his sense of humor.

"I missed a bunch of tournaments," said the tour's answer to Henny Youngman, "but considering all the hospitalization insurance I carry, I figure I wound up leading money winner."

The voluble Trevino said his back troubles were brought on by lifting heavy objects.

"Now," he cracked, "I don't lift anything heavier than a can of Miller Lite."

Wondered a nearby straight man, "Don't you mean Dr. Pepper?"

"Naw," said Trevino. "My contract with Dr. Pepper's up. I'm workin' on a deal with Miller Lite. And I just signed to do commercials for a mattress company and fulfilled my life's ambition. I'll get paid for lyin' down."

For once, though, Trevino was at a loss for clever words. When fans ask him how his back is, he's stumped.

"I get that question several hundred times a day," he said. "Sometimes right after I hit a screaming 2-iron four feet from the hole. People are nice to be concerned about me, but I don't know what to say. I've started answering 'just fine' and letting it go at that."

The question our editors were asked more than any other early in the 1977 season was: "How's Trevino doing—can he come back?" Trevino is a great player and probably the most entertaining hombre in sports, but recovery from back surgery is problematic at best, let alone for a professional athlete who is closer to 40 than 30.

"I came back too soon after the surgery," he admitted. The operation was late in November, and Trevino tried to play again in February. He was weak—he once hit a 2-iron to a green when his playing partners hit 9-irons — and, in pain, he had to leave the tour for further therapy.

"The doctor tried to tell me I'd need a long time to recuperate, but you know me," Trevino said. "I've always rushed everything. If eating dinner takes more than 45 minutes, I have to get up and run around the table. But I'm not hurtin' any more and I'm buildin' my strength back. I ain't through, baby. I'll win again. Ain't no achin' back can stop this cat!"

"You have to wonder if he can play top-level golf again," said fellow superstar Tom Watson. "Lee's thick through that part of the body anyway. I'm not sure he worked as hard as he should have to recondition himself."

Cary Middlecoff, the 1949 and 1956 U.S. Open winner whose career was ended by back surgery, said, "Lee's a super player and he might make it back, but from my experience I know how tough it will be. I was able to play well in one round of a tournament after my operation, sometimes two rounds, occasionally three rounds — but never four rounds. I never regained enough strength in my legs. My back would tighten up. I'm sure surgical techniques have improved since those days, and Lee's operation may not have been as serious as mine. One of my lower discs had fragmented into powder, and they had to take all that out. If Lee has more of a disc left, he's much better off."

Trevino was better off than Middlecoff. The operation that Dr. Antonio Moure, a Houston neursosurgeon, performed on Trevino is called a bilateral lumbar laminectomy, which involves, I am told, disc repair and the removal of bone from the lower spinal canal. Most of the soft nucleus of the offending disc was taken out, but the cartilage and casing were left.

If the class in anatomy will come to order briefly, it will be recalled that we are supported by a spinal column or backbone. Stacked one on top of another in the spinal column are two dozen vertebrae, spool-like bones that allow us to turn and bend. Between the vertebrae are cylindrical layers of soft cartilage that serve as shock absorbers and are called discs.

The lumbar vertebrae are the last five down, in the lower back. It is here that most people have back trouble. (A recent survey finds that lower-back problems are the leading cause of absenteeism in U.S. business and industry.)

The lumbar vertebrae must support the weight of the entire upper half of the body—the price we pay for standing up on our own two feet instead of staying down on all fours like the early vertebrates; the vertebral column still hasn't completely made the adjustment.

Trevino's problem was that the disc between the fourth and fifth vertebrae ruptured and bulged into the spinal canal, the open shaft toward the back of the spinal column, and put painful pressure on the spinal cord.

"He was born with a narrow spinal canal," explains Dr. Moure. "We made the incision in the middle to preserve ligaments and muscles, and opened up the area. There was no arthritis, which makes it less serious. A disc problem like this can reoccur, but probably not for 10 to 15 years."

Dr. Moure discounts speculation on the tour that being hit by lightning at the Western Open in 1975 brought on Trevino's difficulty. Jerry Heard, a victim of the same lightning strike, was sidelined by back pain and considered surgery.

"Lee's condition was chronic," Dr. Moure says. "The lightning may have aggravated it, but it didn't cause it."

Trevino remembers his back first bothering him greatly after he lifted a greens mower out of a pickup truck as a teenager. He says the straw that broke his back came in June of 1976 when he moved a 70-pound potted plant at home.

SuperMex missed the next nine tournaments, including the U.S. and British Opens which he had won twice each, and when he tried to play in the Mexican Open in early November he could barely swing, the pain was so intense.

"I even whiffed a ball — flat whiffed it!" he says. "I had to get relief. Some doctor friends sent me to Dr. Moure because he specializes in back surgery and plays golf. I wasn't confident about it. The only tour player I knew who'd had back surgery was Ron Cerrudo, and he hasn't played well since. But after the operation I got a lot of letters from low-handicap golfers who've had similar surgery and come back to play well, and they perked me up. Ted Williams dropped me a note and said he had the same operation after he quit playing baseball and is able to play golf. He said it'd take time but to stay with it. I've always been a battler. I worked at it."

Trevino did 30 minutes of special exercising each morning and evening and worked up to jogging. At his $600,000 home in New Mexico, just across the border from El Paso and overlooking the Rio Grande River and the new 36-hole Santa Teresa Country Club he owns with friends, Trevino converted his four-car garage into an elaborately equipped gymnasium and built another garage.

In the spring of 1977 he said, "I feel good, and the doc says the only way I can reinjure myself is to lift something heavy. I don't touch that big golf bag, let me tell you. If somebody isn't there to lift it out of the car, I don't play. I'm still a little tight because that scar tissue in there won't stretch. I'm not getting the club back from the ball as far, and I never got it back very far. It can be a problem for a while yet, the doc says.

"I lost 15 pounds—two inches in the legs—and I need more strength. I can't get my legs to work as fast, and I've always been a legs player. I get tired the last few holes in a round. One thing about it, I can play a lot of shots — feathered 3-irons and that sort of stuff—to compensate for losing distance.

"My short game is better than it's been for the last couple of years. My putting's good and my wedge game's much sharper. When you can't play, you lie there and analyze different shots, and I decided to go back to my natural game. I used to hit that 50-yard wedge shot in there low and it'd take one skip and stop. Then I tried to get fancy and float it in, and I couldn't get the ball close to the hole. Now I'm givin' it my caddie-yard swing."

Trevino vowed he could come back, although there was no precedent for a top golfer undergoing back surgery and returning to the top level of the sport. (Craig Wood, the 1941 U.S. Open champion, had a back operation and returned to the tour to play well, but did not win another important title.) The commissioner's office hoped against hope Trevino could win again. "There's only one Lee Trevino," summed up a tour official. "People still flock to Palmer— but they die with Arnie and laugh with Lee." There are plenty of impressive backswings on the tour but precious few players who can make the game — and life in the large—more fun for all of us. Trevino is that rarity, an athlete-entertainer who can.

In the summer of 1977, Trevino won the Canadian Open, believed by some to be the fifth most significant tournament in golf. It was his 20th pro victory and it came against a strong field. He led all four days and shot 280, eight under par, on the scenically rugged, windswept new Glen Abbey course designed by Jack Nicklaus near Toronto. "When you've been hurt bad," said an emotional Trevino, "you want to prove you can win again. This is what my confidence needs."

Lee Buck Trevino, the happy warrior, was back, and how welcome it was. "In his illness and absence," said runner-up Peter Oosterhuis of England, "we forgot how good he is." They operated on his back, but they didn't cut into his determination.

The multi-faceted home life of Lee Trevino allows for scarcely an idle moment and never a dull one. On opposite page, Lee poses with his fleet of antique cars—a Model A Ford, a 1958 Mercedes and a 1954 MG. And he works with the grounds crew at the Santa Teresa Country Club, where he is a part owner, and exercises in his converted garage to strengthen his back and leg muscles. At the immediate left, Lee and his wife Claudia at the family pool table with children (left to right) Tony, Troy and Carl. Lee's as sharp with a pool cue as with a putter. Below, with the $600,000 Trevino home in the background overlooking the Rio Grande, Lee watches gleefully as the kids show off their golf swings. Trevino has moved to Dallas but retains his Santa Teresa interests.

BOB TOSKI: Most modern stars learned to play by technique, unlike the players of yesteryear who learned to play more by feel. Lee Trevino is an exception. He developed his game mainly by feel, and he uses a very unorthodox method. It works for him because he can repeat his swing consistently and his action through the ball is tremendous.

Lee aligns his body left and aims the clubface way left. Then he regrips the club on his backswing. The clubface is shut at the top, which means he has to make an exceptionally strong move with his legs starting down, then "block" the shot to hit it at the target.

Had Trevino been schooled and tutored like Jack Nicklaus when he was young, he might have been as great as Nicklaus.

Lee is quite a player nonetheless, but his swing puts tremendous stress on his back and, in my view, brought on the major surgery he underwent in 1976. His swing does not encourage freedom of motion and flexibility.

Because Lee had a terrible problem with hooking the ball to the

left when he was growing up, he evolved what he calls his "brink of disaster theory." By aligning and aiming to the left, where he fears going, he could not swing to the left at all without hitting a ruinous shot. Knowing he could not let the club-face roll to the left, he disciplined himself to hold the clubface square or slightly open through impact—which takes terrific mental and physical strength—and hit the ball 40 degrees right of where he aimed.

With his body "open" like this, Lee is able to drive forward hard with his legs and square the club-face. He keeps the club going down the target line longer than any good player today, which makes him exceedingly accurate. That's what I mean when I say he "blocks" the shot—he doesn't let the club come back inside the line until the ball is well on its way.

Again, Lee must come through the ball like that or he would hit everything dead left and low. He is a shut-clubface player, and that dictates that he make certain compensations. Most shut-face players aim left because they want to go from shut to square or slightly open

with the face. The open-face player, on the other hand, has a tendency to aim right, then try to manipulate the clubface from open to square or slightly closed. It's also natural if you're a shut-face player to open up the left side of your body as Lee does.

He has the face shut at the top of his swing because he starts with a grip that is comparatively "strong" —his hands are turned too far to his right and under the clubshaft— and then he regrips on his backswing and becomes even stronger.

Keeping the left heel down on the

backswing as much as Lee does contributes to a flat swing plane and a shut clubface at the top.

It helps Lee, on the backswing in particular, that he makes a good, free arm swing to get behind the ball. His shoulders respond to his arms, rather than vice versa. Lee is a good example for all of us here.

With the clubface shut at the top (it would be looking left of target if it were at the bottom of his swing), Lee has to make a strong left-side move on the downswing to be able to play. He has to move very well with his left arm and left leg. If he

allowed his right side to pressure his downswing, he would really hit the ball from left to left, and he'd be lucky to get it off the ground. Trevino is a model left-side player, and this is another aspect of his swing the average player would do well to emulate, while disregarding its more extreme features. All of us right-handers must develop our left side—our weak side—so the right side—our strong side—doesn't take over and dominate the swing.

Notice how Lee moves his left leg and pulls the club forward on the downswing. Lee Trevino has to be more of a legs player than Arnold Palmer, who also shuts the clubface at the top, because Arnold aims right and works his shoulders back around to the left to hit the ball on line. Lee aims left and doesn't overwork his shoulders, so he has to compensate with his leg drive to square up the clubface.

Finally, I want to stress again that this unusual swing works for Lee because he is a great athlete who has hit thousands and thousands of practice balls to groove it. The average golfer couldn't begin to play this way.

HALE IRWIN

The nominations for the toughest competitor on the PGA tour are: Gary Player, for his great pressure shots fired round the world; Jack Nicklaus, for his awesome performances in the big tournaments; Gene Littler, for his victory over cancer and subsequent comeback; Hubert Green, for "rising" the South again, and Hale Irwin, for his blazing determination on every shot every day.

The envelope, please.

The winner is . . . Hale Irwin, for his blazing determination on every shot every day!

Hale Irwin?

He is an unlikely looking candidate, bespectacled, slow to show emotion, outwardly bland. A bank teller, perhaps, or a junior executive in computers. But the toughest competitor on the tour?

Do not be fooled by Irwin's disciplined manner. This is a killer in sheep's clothing—make it cashmere, if you will. Just ask his opponents.

"He really wants to beat your ass," says Dave Hill.

"He really wants to beat your ass," says Roger Maltbie.

"He really wants to beat your ass," says Tom Kite.

These are men who pride themselves on their unwavering determination in a totally individual sport, men who gladly would thrust their heads into the jaws of sharks if it would cut their scores by half a stroke. Yet they openly marvel at the fierceness of Irwin's competitive spirit.

Says an official of the tour field staff, who sees all the weekly tournaments, "Jack Nicklaus is a great competitor who usually can turn it on at the right time. But Jack gears his game for the major tournaments, and occasionally he doesn't get it switched on if the occasion isn't the biggest. With Irwin, every shot is life or death, whether it's the Masters or the Magnolia. He competes like mad in practice rounds. If he gets in trouble, he gets tougher

still. Irwin is after you from the first tee to the 18th green. He's the best competitor on the tour."

Competitiveness in golf can take several forms. There is competition against the course; there is competition against the rest of the field; there is competition against yourself to make the best shots possible. Then there is the transcending competition, if you are good enough, against the greats of history.

Irwin is imbued with all those strains of competitiveness. They run together in his makeup, but he is almost unique in his desire to turn golf into a man-to-man showdown.

The popular refrain on tour is that your opponent is the course, not the other players. Play your own game and ignore the scoreboards. It can be a comforting approach under pressure.

"Garbage!" objects Irwin, who is increasingly outspoken. "Anybody who doesn't look at a scoreboard is crazy. I tell my caddie I want to know where I stand and what the guys near me are doing. Sure you play the course, but I'll play the 18th a lot differently if I'm behind than I will if I'm ahead. If I'm behind, I'll try a long carry over water if there's a 50-50 chance I can make it. If I'm ahead, I won't. We're playing stroke play, but it's usually head-to-head if you're in contention down the stretch."

Not surprisingly, Irwin won the Piccadilly World Match Play Championship in Britain twice, before it became the Colgate World Match Play, and got to the semifinals in 1977. His composed intensity has made him an out-and-out hero to the British, who prefer to coat their desires and needs with a layer of decorum.

"He has tremendous drive which he channels into concentration," says British star Peter Oosterhuis, who was flogged by Irwin 9 and 8 in a 36-hole first-round match in the 1975 Piccadilly. "He gets mad, but unlike most of us he turns his anger to his advantage. In the '74 Piccadilly he played Tony Jacklin in the semifinals. Jacklin was the native son and the crowd favorite. The match was close. Then Irwin missed a short putt on the 14th, and some of the fans clapped. He was furious. He birdied the next two holes and blew Tony out of the match."

Another time in the Piccadilly, Irwin was in the process of closing out Gary Player. Irwin led 2-up with two holes to play. On the 17th green, Player missed the putt that represented his last chance, and knocked Irwin's ball away, in effect conceding the match.

The announcer informed the crowd that Irwin had won 2 and 1. "It should be 3 and 1," Irwin retorted. "I would have made that last putt."

Somewhat surprisingly, Irwin would not choose to convert the U.S. tour to match play, it being the growing shame of American professional golf that match play, the original form of the game, has been allowed to lapse here. "There are too many inequities in match play," he says. "Match play doesn't consistently reward the steady player. Like me."

Irwin wins tournaments by shooting around par on difficult courses such as Butler National in Chicago,

where he has won the Western Open, and Riviera, where he has won the Los Angeles Open, and Harbour Town, where he has won the Heritage, and Winged Foot, where he won the 1974 U.S. Open on perhaps the most devilish test of golf ever set up by the U.S. Golf Association. The challenge of an arduous course, like the challenge of a formidable opponent, turns Irwin on. He almost invariably finishes in the top 10 in major events.

His game is built for major-tournament courses. Generally straight off the tee, he also has the facility to scramble and save pars if he gets into trouble; his peers consider him the most adept on tour from 100 yards in.

"My swing has definitely improved in the last few years," Irwin says. "I used to lay the club off too flat coming back, then have to manipulate it with my hands into a more upright plane at the top. Now I stay pretty much in the same plane. I think I have a good swing, and I'm confident that I know my swing and can fix it if something goes out of whack. I literally have been my own teacher through the years—I haven't had a teaching pro to go back to.

"Until recently I couldn't draw the ball—work it from right to left. I've learned to do that. Experience pays off, but you have to be able to keep developing your game at the same time you're competing for a living, week after week, and that isn't easy.

"Winning the Open gave me the confidence I needed. I won it the hard way, and that convinced me I could step up to any shot from here on in and not have to shy away from it. I was one stroke ahead at the 17th hole, but I drove into the rough and had to hack a 4-wood out of bad stuff and then save par with a 10-foot putt. Any win helps you, but that one made me. I mean, I was on the ropes, trying to throw away the biggest title in the country. I told myself, 'Get yourself together, pull out what you need to do the job.' The 18th hole was the closest to perfect I've ever played. I hit an excellent drive and a dead-straight 2-iron and almost made the putt—under the toughest conditions you can find. At Winged Foot, a two-shot lead is nothing, and I knew there'd be no flukey way to get the ball on the fairway and on the green on that 18th hole. It just had to be done, and I did it. The feeling I had of pride and elation is impossible to describe."

Says Steve Reid, a former tour player now working in the commissioner's office, "Irwin has a complete game—all the little in-between shots, the shots that aren't really pitch shots and aren't really chips and aren't really in any of the textbooks. He can invent a shot to fit a new situation, and he can do it on the last day of a major tournament. But his biggest asset is his attitude. He never gives up. He *cares* so much you can't believe it. It *truly* hurts him to lose. He *can't* stand to lose."

Adds Roger Maltbie, an intrigued student of human nature, "If he has a bad day, he'll vow to himself that he isn't going to let it happen again. He'll go hit 300 range balls until it gets dark. He'll invariably shoot a low score the next day. I think he expects more of himself than any-body else out here."

I asked Irwin during the Masters Tournament if he could explain his competitiveness. We were sitting in the dining room at a corner table underlooking a television set that carried closed-circuit coverage of the action, eating steak sand-wiches and peaches, the specialty of the house. Before he answered, Irwin intently watched Jack Nick-laus assess and sink a 10-foot putt.

"Jack's the target," Irwin said. "I'm out to beat him, here and everyplace else. I respect him, but I'm sure not afraid of him. I asked him here once if he was ready to defend his unprecedented fifth Masters championship. He said, 'Yeah, and if you guys don't play well, I'll make it six.' He's a tre-mendous competitor. That made me want to go get him."

Of his own competitiveness Irwin said, "I refuse to accept less than what I'm capable of achieving, at any time. My goal every year is to play better than the year before.

"I'm always looking for a com-petitive stimulus. I was paired with Lou Graham today, and he was playing well, so I played harder to try to catch him. I've always been that way. When I was a little kid I would pretend I had a shot to win the Masters. Something to make me try my best. Maybe it's in my genes. My father and brother are the same way."

Irwin's father, an excavation con-tractor and a low-handicap week-end golfer, first cut down clubs for Hale to swing when he was 3 and the family lived in Baxter Springs, Kansas. Hale Sr. remembers his

29

The gritty Irwin was the only player who never missed a 36-hole cutoff in 1977.

son practicing all day as a youngster: "I'd stick around for an hour and then leave because I was getting tired just watching him."

Says Hale's younger brother Phil, a bank manager in Boulder, Colorado, and, like Hale, a former cocaptain of the U. of Colorado football squad, "He worked at golf harder than I worked at digging ditches when we were kids out of school in the summer. He'd get a lot of needling from other kids because he was playing golf and they were working. But to Hale, golf was his job. He worked at the game 10 hours a day and knew he wanted to be a pro. Our parents always stressed doing things correctly. They were pleasant and patient with us, but we got the message, and they set the example. Hale would spend days on one shot until he got it right. I think he wanted to please our parents.

"There couldn't be a more competitive person in the world," continues Phil, "unless it's me. We don't show it. We were taught that it isn't right to show your competitiveness because it can look egotistical and you can hurt people. We were taught to do our best but to get along with people."

When Hale was 14, the Irwins moved to Boulder. There he was exposed to tournament golf for the first time, and his friend and rival was Dick Anderson, now an outstanding defensive back for the Miami Dolphins. The two were all-round athletes in high school and then moved on to the state university in Boulder.

In football they teamed at the safety positions, Anderson, a bigger, more natural athlete, Irwin, medium sized, and not particularly fast either. But Irwin was willing. Oh, how he was willing.

"He had a sense for where the ball was going," recalls Anderson. "He loved to dart up and crack a ballcarrier head-on at the line of scrimmage. A really fierce competitor, he didn't have great physical ability, but he could have made it in the pros. You don't find many competitors like him in any sport."

One fall day in 1965, Colorado was battling powerful Oklahoma. Colorado led 7-0 with time left for only one play in the first half, but Oklahoma had the ball at the Colorado one-yard line. Worse yet, Colorado had changed its lineup, and when Irwin checked his team's defense as the play was about to start, he noticed that Colorado was a man short. Nobody was lined up in the crucial middle-guard position. The Oklahoma quarterback no-

ticed the same thing. The 175-pound Irwin bolted into the hole in the line, the ball was snapped, the play thundered right at him, and he stacked it up short of the end zone. It was the big play in a 13-0 Colorado victory.

Les Fowler, the Colorado golf coach, encouraged Irwin to play football as well as golf. "I thought playing football would add to his competitive instincts and his physical condition," Fowler says. "I think it did. Besides, he was the kind of aggressive, well-put-together kid who never got hurt."

"Not only that," quips Irwin. "Golf got me out of spring football practice. Spring football was the hardest thing I've ever done. I went to Colorado on a football scholarship and was obligated to go to spring drills my first year. But the rules said that if you had a spring sport, you didn't have to attend football practice. Golf got me off the hook after my freshman year. I imagine I'd have won sooner on the tour — it took me 3½ years — if I'd played more golf while I was in college but football was a good experience."

Adds Les Fowler, "It's significant to me that Hale's aggressiveness on the golf course didn't show up in gambling play, even then. His competitiveness showed in the pride he took in executing shots impeccably."

Irwin says, "I've never been a birdie machine. I don't have the talent to turn it on like Nicklaus or Weiskopf. I learned early that I'd have to manage what I have intelligently. I have a degree in marketing from Colorado, and I think that

31

background helps me make sound decisions. I try to make pressure and tension work for me. I want the adrenalin to be flowing. I think sometimes we try so hard to be cool, calm and collected we forget what we're doing. There's nothing wrong with being charged up if it's controlled."

Occasionally, there is a dark side to Irwin's competitiveness. While he is generally well liked on the tour, some players resent his single-mindedness. "I admire his ability," says one young pro, "but his competitiveness wears on you."

Says a critical veteran, "He wants to win so badly he can be a crybaby on the course. He'll lip out a putt, and walking to the next tee he'll say, 'Did you see that? No way that ball can go left!' He should realize that you couldn't care less. A lot of players aren't eager to be paired with him."

Recently Irwin has seemed much more relaxed, if no less intent on becoming the best player in the game. At one point during a major match, Irwin came off the course and said, "Maybe I'm trying too hard — but that's the only way I know." But an hour later he was analyzing himself in a more reflective and mellow mood.

"I'm trying never to get mad at outside influences—the gallery, a bad bounce, the weather. I'm pointing the finger at myself. It's taken time for me to get to know my game and myself, but I'm getting there. If some problem or anxiety is bothering me, I try to bring it out, dissect it logically and deal with it. That's why I'm playing better. I'm more comfortable with myself. I'm more me."

Which brings us to Irwin's supposedly chronic image problem. He has a non-image as far as the public is concerned. "The trick is to get people to know the guy behind the glasses and the visor," says Hughes Norton, who handles Irwin's business for the Mark McCormack conglomerate. "He's great dinner company, but that doesn't transmit on the golf course."

Irwin's thoughtfulness and articulateness do make him great dinner company, particularly for an athlete. The vocabulary of the typical professional athlete barely extends beyond the inside lexicon of of his sport. Irwin can make you think.

I once asked him what sets a pro golfer apart from athletes in other major sports. He briefly contemplated his navel and then responded to my leading question like a true champion. He coined a catchy word.

"The only-ness," he answered.

I found it a marvelous reply. Golf often has been called a lonely game, but to speak of a player's only-ness is to add needed dimension. It is a word that comes at once from the stomach, the heart and the head, speaking to us meaningfully on several levels.

"You're all by yourself out there in the center of the fairway with only a small ball and your psyche," Irwin said. "It's a long way to the hole. There are no lines regulating play. You can rely on your caddie

His fellow players consider Irwin the most dangerous man on tour from 100 yards on in to the green.

for the yardage, but only one person can hit the shot—you."

Irwin contrasted the only-ness of golf with the team aspect of football, America's most popular spectator sport. "In a game like football, there's always something to stimulate you. I wasn't very big, and I felt that every play was for my life. In golf you don't get stimulated by a whack in the kisser. Your stimulation has to come from little things . . . a good bounce, a good lie at a crucial time. Then you tell yourself maybe your luck isn't all bad after all.

"Golf is our most sophisticated sport. On the tour you almost never hit a full shot. Every swing demands a different degree of control. It's very wearing emotionally. I'm most relaxed late in a round, when I'm tired."

As well as he expresses himself, Irwin cannot help his marketing people project a new image for him. "I've thought for a while that maybe I should find a gimmick to be known for," he says, "but I'm not going to turn phony. You and I have two strikes against us these days because we wear glasses and we aren't blond. But I'm not going to switch to contact lenses and dye my hair to get attention. Your photographer suggested I grow a beard. I don't know . . . I can wear red, but it looks different on me than it does on Johnny Miller because of what people want to see. I don't get hung up on it. My image is appealing to my wife and my friends and people who know the game well.

"I think I've been anonymous to the people who follow Jack Nicklaus, Arnold Palmer and Lee Trevino. I don't think I'm anonymous to the player on tour or to the low-handicap amateur, the person who keeps abreast of the golfing scene."

Irwin also is undisturbed by the myth of conservatism that has built up around him.

"I don't consider myself conservative," he says. "The people who know me don't consider me conservative. If others want to believe I am, that's fine. I hope they don't, but I'm not going to go over to them and say, 'Hey, I'm not conservative.'

"When I'm around somebody I don't know, I want to cast myself as a professional, because that's what I feel I am. I want to present an air of a guy who knows what he's talking about and has some common sense. But when I'm with people I know, I can clown, if it's the natural thing for me to do at the time. I do things that are spontaneous, not thought out. Like when I holed the final putt at the 1974 Open and threw the ball . . . the ball was out of my hand so fast I didn't even know where it went. It was gone before I realized it.

"Some people plan things like that, but phoniness is not my bag. I just figure that if I get to know enough people, they'll realize I'm not really a closed-up little guy who has a tax-accountant look about him. I know I'm not an immortal—but maybe by now I'm at least a slight household name."

It should encourage Irwin on the matter of his image, or lack of one, to remember that Jack Nicklaus had the same problem earlier in his career. Nicklaus built a solid follow-ing mainly through the sheer force of his ability, with a little help from his dietitian. "Now he has a large following made up of students of the game," points out Al Geiberger. "Irwin could develop the same kind of following."

"He should play very well for a long time," says Bob Goalby. "He's thin in the waist and doesn't look as though he'll ever get heavy. He can rip at the ball and not worry about losing it to the left. And I can't conceive of him losing interest."

Lee Trevino flatly predicts that Irwin will go down as one of the all-time greats. "He's the most underrated player in the game and he's just scratching the surface of his talent," Trevino says, adding, just to make it unanimous, that Irwin is one helluva competitor for a man with fair skin.

Maybe Hale Irwin has an image problem, but it ought to be enough that he is the toughest competitor on the tour. It's more than enough for his opponents, and I don't mean the golf courses.

Even a serious-minded golfer like Hale Irwin can have a good time at a zoo, and here Hale and his wife Sally frolic with their children Becky and Steven at the famed St. Louis Zoo. On opposite page, Hale and the kids grill steaks and play ball in the backyard. Irwin is said to be the best outdoor cook on the tour.

BOB TOSKI: The thing I admire most about Hale Irwin's swing never shows in pictures. That is his willingness to work hard and improve his swing. I don't believe anyone ever has put more effort into developing a good swing than Hale. It isn't easy to make substantial changes once you start playing the tour—you're inclined to keep playing with a swing that isn't really good enough, because the money's so big you don't want to take the time off to practice. Hale has never hesitated to do what he thought was best for his swing over the long term, even if it cost him a few temporary gains. I have great

respect for him.

Until the last two or three years, Hale aimed too far to the right of his target and then "laid the club off" on his backswing. By that I mean he took the club away from the ball too much inside the target line and around his body, instead of bringing it straighter back and up. As a result, he had to jerk the club up into a different plane to get it in a functional position at the top of his swing, and he tended to compensate at the start of his downswing by "coming over the top"— looping the club too much from the outside back over to his left to get it on the target line. He manipulated

the club with his hands too much. His leg action had to be tremendous.

We still see some of that deficiency in this swing sequence, but by and large Hale has retrained himself to swing in a much simpler manner. He swings the club back and forward on pretty much the same plane nowadays, and he doesn't use his hands excessively starting down. He squares the club at impact with much less recovery action than before.

I like his posture. He is out over the ball with a good tilt in his upper body, and his arms hang so they can swing freely. His weight is toward the balls of his feet and he doesn't have too much flex in his knees the way many weekend players do—just a slight flex so he isn't stiff.

He starts with a relatively flat left-wrist position at address, and pretty much retains it throughout his swing. This straight-line relationship of the left forearm, wrist and hand was at the heart of the square-to-square method, but many people misunderstood it and thought we were talking about the clubface looking at the target throughout the swing or something. Good players like Irwin start with the flat left wrist, and at the top it's flat and at

impact it's flat. That's why they strike the ball squarely with consistency. There's no breakdown of the left wrist during the swing. If all golfers would start the swing with a flat left wrist and concentrate on keeping it flat at the top and at the bottom, they'd be on the way to hitting the ball straighter.

I also like the way Hale lets his left heel come off the ground on his backswing. With the left heel coming up, he has more flexibility to work his left knee and get his weight behind the ball at the top of his swing. I see many, many higher handicap players who are afraid to let the left heel come off

the ground. They get hung up on the left side on the backswing and can't get any movement or support from the left leg on the downswing. Their weight goes forward when it should go back, and back when it should go forward. I guess they're afraid that if they let the left side ride back with the right side on the backswing, they'll lose control. But they fail to realize how important mobility and flexibility are in the swing. I don't want them to sway away from the ball with the body, but they have to learn to swing up and around and get behind the ball at the top.

I'm surprised that Hale's back-

swing plane is as flat as it is, considering that his left heel is off the ground that much. In this swing he has to be using a little too much hand and wrist action still, because with the heel off the ground that much he should be able to swing his arms upward much easier.

Starting the downswing, he shifts his weight quickly but smoothly back over to his left side, which is good. The arms swing down freely and the legs work well. He does a good job of retaining the angle between the shaft of the club and the lead arm until he's near the hitting area, then it releases for an almost effortlessly powerful hit.

At impact, Irwin pretty much exemplifies the three key positions I see good players getting into and poorer players not. His head has remained relatively steady throughout the swing—it has swiveled but hasn't moved laterally appreciably—and it is in basically the same place it was at address. So are the left arm and left heel, which he has replanted. He can swing the left arm from inside the line out toward the target, and that means straight shots, not just for four or five holes a round but for 13, 15, 18 holes. That's what it's all about.

41

TOM WATSON

It was one of those searingly hot, summery afternoons when you could fry an egg on the clubhouse veranda and breathing was an effort, and Thomas Sturges Watson, the player of the year, was probably the most uncomfortable person on the Muirfield Village course. Something he ate in a Columbus cafeteria the night before had turned his stomach into an out-of-control roller coaster, and every few holes he suddenly had to disappear into the trees with a stricken look on his face. Fortunately, it was a thickly treed course.

"He feels awful," said his wife Linda, who walks every step of the tour with him. "He didn't sleep last night and he can't wait to get back to the motel and lie down."

Watson strode falteringly onto the last green in good position for a birdie despite his discomfort, a birdie that would move him near the lead in the 1977 Memorial Tournament. But his sidehill putt careened past the hole, and he missed the five-footer coming back.

The three-putt bogey made Watson so angry he forgot his illness and stalked straight to the practice green. There, with his exhausted young caddie sitting cross-legged behind the hole to retrieve the balls, he stroked, over and over, the five-foot putt he had missed on the final hole—113 times by actual journalistic count.

Finally, his light-colored orange shirt drenched with perspiration, Watson grunted in a semblance of satisfaction and went to the locker room. "I was trying to get behind the ball more, to see the line better," he said as he changed shoes. "And I was trying to hit through the ball. I'm not putting well, and it makes me mad to finish that way, turning a birdie into a bogey."

Watson's penetrating green eyes were blazing with enough intensity to light up an entire city in a blackout. Johnny Miller, whose own dedication blows hot and cold, has said of Watson, "I played with him a few years ago, before he was winning all these tournaments, and I knew right away he was going to be No. 1. You could see it in his eyes."

Watson's eyes give away the unrelenting determination behind his relaxed manner. They tell the observant that he is going to let nothing within his control stop him from becoming a great champion. Jack Nicklaus also saw that riveting quality early on. "He knows exactly where he's going," Nicklaus said of Watson a few years ago. "He has great ability and super confidence."

Now Nicklaus faces the most formidable challenge of his legendary career from Watson, who turned him back to win both the Masters and the British Open in 1977. In the Masters, Nicklaus charged magnificently from behind, but Watson didn't rattle. In the British, Nicklaus raced off to a three-stroke lead early the last day, but the plucky Watson played magnificently to overtake him. "I gave it my best shot both times," laments Nicklaus. "I'm tired of giving it my best shot and it isn't good enough."

It has been accepted for years on the tour that when Jack is at his best, as he usually is in the important tournaments, he is unbeatable; when he's off his game, someone else has a chance to win for a change. Watson is forcing a rethinking of that appraisal. When Nicklaus shot a rousing 66 the last day at Augusta, Watson shot an equally rousing 67. When Nicklaus shot an inspired 66 the last day at Turnberry, Watson, playing head to head with him, shot an even more inspired 65. Tenacious Tom is not the least bit intimidated by Big Jack, and Big Jack must find that more than a little frustrating.

Of course, it is easy to forget, in the excitement of the present, that Nicklaus has been challenged frequently by a player who puts it all together for a year—gets "in the zone" as the tennis players say—and that Jack has responded with surpassing results. In 1971, remember, Lee Trevino won every National Open but the Siberian in a span of about four weeks, and was trumpeted as the man who was going to replace Nicklaus. The next year Nicklaus won seven tournaments and set a money record. In 1974, Johnny Miller broke 65 approximately as often as he brushed his teeth, and won eight tournaments. Everyone thought he was the best golfer in the world at the time. The next year Nicklaus won five tournaments, including two of the majors that mostly elude Miller, and that was that.

Nicklaus, with his 16 major championships and ongoing excellence, remains the standard against which everyone else, including Watson, is measured. Watson is the first to agree. "It's satisfying to finish ahead of Jack twice in big tournaments," he says, "but it's one thing to have a big year and quite another to attain real greatness like Jack's. My goal is to reach that kind of greatness."

Watson is nearly 10 years Jack's junior, which on the golf tour is tantamount at least to a generation, and it is difficult to find an insider who doesn't believe the

best is still to come for him. Looking at his comparatively brief six-year pro career from an overview, he has made startling progress in all respects, and you are left with the firm impression that his improvement has been carefully programmed and arduously brought about.

Says Raymond Floyd, "Golf is like any other profession—you don't get anything for nothing. Tom Watson didn't just appear out of nowhere to win two major championships in 1977. He's built him-

A strong booster of junior golf, Watson has a close rapport with youngsters, as evidenced at events like this Insurance Youth Classic.

self to a peak for the past five years. Every time I'd go to the practice tee, he'd be there. Every time I'd go to the putting clock, he'd be there. I'd say he worked harder at his game than anybody else out there in that time. When you work hard on your game and prepare yourself well for competition, you play better. When you play better,

45

you gain confidence. It's a snow-ball effect, and if you're talented enough you have a year like he had. He's good enough and determined enough to keep improving."

Watson weighs and measures his words closely before answering questions, then replies in a steady stream of articulateness, his luminous eyes locking yours to attention. The eyes smolder out of a compellingly handsome face topped by coppery hair and marred and made real only by a light sprinkling of freckles and a thin scar that runs beneath his lower lip. ("One day when I was a kid I was trying to do a watermelon —that's a crazy dive—into a swimming pool at a country club in Kansas City, and my head hit the water and drove my teeth through my lip.") Watson comes from a comfortable country club background — the overworked analogies to Huck Finn are about as apt as likening Jimmy Carter to the Farmer in the Dell—but he is deceptively tough and resilient, as his reshaping of his swing shows.

"I've been relaxing my right side better and making a bigger shoulder turn. I have more left-side leadership in my swing, and it flows better. I owe a great deal to Byron Nelson, who worked with me before the 1977 season at his ranch in Texas. My dad, who is a good golfer himself, used to tell me Byron was the finest iron player of all time, and I can see why. He still hits it incredibly straight."

Many of us see in Watson's swing a new compactness as well as a new smoothness and assurance. Before, he took the driver back well below horizontal; today, the club is just about parallel to the ground. Tommy Bolt, one of the game's all-time shot-makers, says, "With that firmer action, he'll win a bunch more tournaments. He's made an adjustment that Ben Crenshaw hasn't made. Crenshaw's swing is still too big and loose to be repeatable."

Elaborates John Mahaffey, who has been Watson's closest friend on the tour, "Tom's like Ben Hogan in that he isn't afraid to change his swing. He's made a change every year he's been on tour, I think. Most pros are afraid to do that— they're afraid they'll play poorly for a week or two and miss a good pay check. Tom's not impulsive— he won't make a change until he's convinced something isn't working —but once he decides to make it, he'll go ahead and put it to the test under competitive pressure, which is the only way to find out if it'll take."

Steve Reid, the tour's television coordinator and a former pro player, gives further perspective to Watson's resolute improvement: "He probably could have won more before this year if he'd been less geared to developing his game for the long haul. He could have resorted to baling-wire, Band-Aid cures to get through the week, but he didn't compromise. He had faith in his ability to build for the future. The 1977 Crosby tournament was a good example. He came to the last hole with a two-stroke lead. That's a rugged finishing hole, with the ocean on the left all the way. He had to be nervous, and he could have taken a 3-wood

and shot away from the water. Instead, he nailed the driver right down the left center.

"The thing I like about his swing," enthuses Reid, "is that he always turns it loose—always releases, even on little half shots. He never blocks a shot. He has no limitations, because he finds his limitations and fixes them."

Watson is far from satisfied with his swing, improved though it is, and has found more limitations to fix. "I need to keep the ball down and draw it," he says, his eyes smoldering with intentness. "I hit the ball awfully high, which can be a problem in the wind. I'd like to hit more of a boring shot that would go lower but still bite on the green. Shortening my swing and driving my legs more has helped. Now I need to flatten my plane somewhat. I hear all the talk about a 45-degree plane being ideal for everybody, but as far as I'm concerned that's too flat. I want to be between 60 and 70 degrees. I've always been very upright, but I've let myself get a little too upright, and it's hard for me to move the ball to the left or the right, high or low, from the same plane. I've always been a natural right-to-left player, but you have to broaden your shot-making scope. I've always admired Sam Snead's swing —he can hit all the shots from the same plane, without forcing anything."

Until last year, Watson's swing tended to quicken under the unrelenting pressure of a close finish. He lost some tournaments he could have won, including the 1974 and '75 U.S. Opens, and a few callous writers speculated that he was a "choker" who came apart in the clutch.

I'm not sure what "choking" means, but if it means lack of character and courage under fire, Watson is not guilty of it—his recent record ought to be proof enough that he is a superior competitor. Watson himself says, "I think everybody chokes. Usually you choke when you're swinging at the ball poorly but you're still in contention. You choke because you know you have to make good shots with a swing that is only 50 percent effective. If you have confidence in your swing, you don't choke."

Possibly there were other considerations in Watson's case. Al Geiberger says, "I think I know how Tom thinks, and in the past when he got in position to win he sometimes would get so excited he'd shoot himself out of contention, he wanted to win so badly. Now he keeps himself on a more even keel emotionally." Frank Beard figures Watson has lost tournaments he could have won because of his aggressive tactics. "He's not a choker, but you can't go for the flag *all* the time," Beard says. Bob Goalby concurs and adds, "He goes full bore and doesn't back off, so he's going to goof up in crucial situations more than someone who is conservative. That doesn't make him a choker."

Jim Simons suggests a closer study of Watson's record if we must persist in talking about choking. "Look at the courses where he supposedly choked," Simons says. "Winged Foot. Medinah. Harbour Town. Sawgrass. Those are tremendously exacting courses where every shot has to be executed almost perfectly or you're staring at a high number. You just like to be in a spot to choke on courses like that."

You have to get there to choke and you have to care deeply to choke, if we must use the graceless term. Watson, to his credit, did not once lose his composure in the face of repeated questioning about his intestinal fortitude, and he went through two painful cycles of it, once in 1975 before he won the British Open for the first time and again last spring before he won the Masters. I remember him saying early in the week at Carnoustie in 1975, "You have to lose major championships before you can win them. It's the price you pay for maturing. The more times you can put yourself in pressure situations, the better off you are. It's a learning experience that's worth a fortune. You have to keep thinking affirmatively and looking forward."

Last year the renewed conjecture about his play under pressure bothered Watson more than he let on. "It's garbage!" he exclaimed once, his eyes on fire. "That kind of reputation can ruin a man's career. I've been there before and I've lost, but I've also worked hard to improve. I've never considered myself a choker, and I don't understand that kind of talk from others."

If Watson can sound like a psychology graduate of Stanford University, it's only because he is. He credits his exposure to positive-thinking texts with helping him to learn to relax under pressure, but says his college major has been overemphasized in relation to golf.

"Studying psychology isn't that relevant to the tour. I took mostly general courses in group psychology—I'd be a great gallery marshal. What college really prepares you for is graduate school. You can be a smart golfer without a college degree, and you can have a doctorate and pull the wrong club out of the bag. Course management is the difference between shooting 80 and shooting 74, and you pick that up from experience and instinct. Selecting the best route out of trouble, even if it's only going to get you a double bogey, is a big part of it, and you don't learn that in a college classroom.

"In college I developed self-discipline and a greater sense of self-awareness. I went from a small private high school in Kansas to a big university in California — from a closed environment to an open one — and the whole experience helped me grow."

Watson is careful not to sound intellectual around the tour, where reading anything more challenging than the morning paper can be considered pretty heavy stuff. One afternoon this year a locker room discussion centered on sex, as locker room discussions have over the years, and Watson piped up, "The average male thinks about sex every 15 minutes."

"What's your source?" Johnny Miller wanted to know.

"Hollywood Squares," said Watson with an impish chuckle.

Did Watson, with his inquiring mind (he has been called the only liberal on the tour, and reportedly was the lone pro to vote for George McGovern in 1972), ever seriously consider a career other than golf? His father is a prosperous insurance man, his brother a lawyer. It is easy to see Tom as an up-and-coming junior executive who would run the company in five years.

"During college I tried to give myself a chance at other things, but my senior year I decided to go where my talent was greatest — that was golf. I've always liked the individual challenge golf presents. You're your own man and you're as good as you can make yourself. I could see myself as a businessman eventually, but right now I don't allow myself the luxury of thinking about other careers. Golf is my profession—what I'm trying to be the best at—and it's a consuming one."

Away from the course, Watson is zealously protective of his time and privacy. He does only a few corporate outings, and is taking his time sorting through the dozens of extracurricular offers that have been gushing in. He is his own business manager, after an unsatisfactory trial period with the giant Mark McCormack organization. His wife Linda, a bright, attractive, aggressive young woman he began going with in high school, is his peripatetic bookkeeper and travel agent, and her brother, Charles Rubin, a Kansas City lawyer, handles his contracts.

"Time is more important to him

than money," says Rubin. "Tom is dedicated to improving his golf—I've never seen anyone as dedicated to anything as Tom is to golf—and he also wants to be sure he takes time to be with his family and relax from the new pressures."

Finding time for himself is increasingly difficult for Watson, one part of whom is a very private person. ("We don't know all of Tom Watson," says Tony Jacklin. "We only know what he wants us to know. He says all the right things to all the right people, but there's a deeper side to the man.") Watson is running out of places to seclude himself and is concerned about the loss of freedom.

He says, "When I turned pro I wasn't thinking about what could happen if I became a celebrity. The travel is wearing enough, and then there are all the other distractions and demands on your time. You keep telling yourself you'll live a normal life, but this is not a normal life. Of course, I suppose if I were in business back in Kansas City I'd want to be on the tour. I guess you always want what you don't have."

To keep his psychic balance, Watson likes to disappear from the public eye for extended hunting and fishing trips, particularly toward the end of the year. "I like to play a lot early and then get completely away for a while," he says. "When I was growing up in Kansas, in Prairie Village near Kansas City, I'd always end the season on Labor Day and not play again till spring. It kept me from getting jaded, and after Christmas my interest would start to pick up again.

I played other sports—I played guard on the basketball team in high school and quarterback on the football team, but at 5'9" and 160 pounds I was too small for college ball. I was a good outside shot in basketball and a pretty good running quarterback, with the benefit of a 300-pound center who ran interference for me. We live in Overland Park now, and I still enjoy Kansas. We have a lot of friends there and I love to hunt in the fall—quail, duck, pheasant."

Recently Watson and his brother-in-law, Chuck Rubin, went on a fishing trip to Canada to escape the frenetic pace of the tour, 200 miles above civilization in upper Manitoba. "The tranquility was great for him," Rubin says. "Everyone should get away from his work that way once or twice a year. We flew in by bush plane, and there was nobody else on the lake. You could drink out of the lake, the water was so clear and clean. At night the only light was the moon setting on the lake—there were no city lights on the horizon. The only sounds were the wind and an occasional wolf."

Watson returned to the tour refreshed and invigorated. Again he was all golf. I recall a locker room exchange he had with Tom Weiskopf, a straightforward but amiable dialogue that told much about Tom Watson.

Weiskopf complained of being bored with golf.

Watson said, "I get bored with the travel, but not the people or the game." His eyes turned steely. "If I ever got to that point," he said with convincing finality, "I'd quit."

With much the same intensity and dedication that characterize his golf, Tom Watson has taken up flying. He poses above with a Beechcraft Sundowner in his home town of Kansas City, Ks., and below discusses flight plans with his instructor, Harold King. At left, Tom and Linda Watson share a few of the private moments that are increasingly difficult to come by. Linda travels the tour with her husband and walks every round with him.

BOB TOSKI: Tom Watson's swing path is outstanding, and I want you to appreciate why.

Most weekend players do not swing the clubhead on the right route. Golfers of my generation, in particular, were often told to make an "inside-out" swing. They were taught to swing the clubhead into the ball from inside the target line to outside the target line. That piece of advice may have ruined more golfers over the years than any other single thought.

On a good swing path like Watson's, the clubhead comes down from inside the line, travels along the line through impact, then moves back inside the line again. The clubhead does not go outside the line at any point in the swing.

Watson sets up so he can swing the club on the proper path. He looks as if he's aiming left of his target, but he's actually "parallel left" as we phrase it at our Golf Digest Instruction Schools. His club is aimed at the target. His body is aligned left of target but on an imaginary line that would run parallel to his target line. That's consistent. Many average players

align the body at the target, which means the clubhead is going to point way right of target and the swing path is going to be inside-out if they don't drastically reroute the club. They have to overwork their hands coming down, and anything can happen.

Watson's swing path is good because it's natural and simple. That's why his swing looks so effortless and uncomplicated.

I approve of his address position, with a couple of exceptions. He appears to have a little more rigidity in his left arm than he needs. I don't like to see too much tension in the upper part of the left arm, because it will restrict the flow of the arm away from the ball and you're tempted to get too quick with the hands. I would rather see the left arm hanging more freely, with just enough tension in the last three fingers of the left hand to control the club. I believe Tom does concentrate on those pressure points in the left hand.

The other minus in his address position is that he looks to have more weight on his left side than I would suggest. With the weight on

the left side, you can be prone to snatch the club away from the ball too abruptly and make a reverse weight shift. Tom's hands are a little far forward, rather than inside the left knee where I like them, and that is part of the reason he has his weight left.

But his ball position is forward, just inside his left heel, and that gets his head behind the ball and helps him shift his weight to his right on the backswing. Also, his right side is relaxed so that his left side — his lead side — can control the swing as it should.

He swings the club up primarily with his arms, and his hands react to his arms. If the hands move first, you break down.

Tom's swing is shorter and firmer than it was, because his right leg is resisting better on the backswing. He doesn't let the knee sway. Here, he still is getting the club below horizontal at the top, because he is letting the right knee bow to his right somewhat. I'd rather see his right knee stay where it was at address.

But his upper-body coil is very impressive. His back is facing the tar-

get at the top. That's the result of his arms swinging up and around his body. He makes a full shoulder turn, yes, but his arms lead on the backswing and his shoulders follow. In a good swing, the arms travel 180 degrees and the shoulders only 90. Think about that the next time somebody tells you to concentrate on turning your shoulders.

Good players like Watson come down into the ball from inside—the clubhead is moving from inside the line of play—by driving the left leg laterally, which supports the swing-ing of the left arm and keeps the head in position behind the ball. A lot of average golfers try to stay behind the ball and succeed—but they swing the clubhead outside the target line. They're behind the ball, but they're not inside it.

At impact, Watson's head is at least as far behind the ball as it was at address. Driving the lower body forward tilts the upper body back.

After impact, the clubhead moves down the target line and then back inside the line. It's this enviable swing path that impresses me most about Watson.

RAYMOND FLOYD

I first got to know Raymond Floyd in 1969, which was a very good year both for him and for Pouilly Fuissé, his favorite liquid refreshment. It was late August and the North Beach section of San Francisco, home of the topless night spot and Carol Doda, the original silicone girl, was ablaze with brightly lit marquees that proclaimed: "WELCOME HOME, RAY FLOYD."

The owner of The Condor Club was asked by a well-lubricated convention goer if this Ray Floyd was his new go-go dancer. No, said the owner tolerantly, Ray Floyd wasn't a go-go dancer, he was a good ole boy from Carolina and a golfer, a fine one. He had just won the Professional Golfers' Association Championship in Dayton, Ohio, and he was a familiar and popular figure in the smoky, dimly lit North Beach clubs. He once owned an all-girl topless band, the Ladybirds.

"WELCOME HOME, RAY FLOYD."

Floyd considered the notices the supreme tribute. These were his people, and he was proud to have returned the PGA to the bacchanalian tradition of Walter Hagen, who won it five times between magnums of champagne, spent money as if life were a Monopoly game, and was an odds-on favorite of the ladies.

A devoted bachelor, Floyd was the latter-day party boy of golf, and he led the tour in late hours. Asked the color of his eyes, he once said, "They're usually pretty red." His fellow touring professionals talked with awe of "Floyd's girls." He flew them in for tournaments in out-of-the-way places like Augusta, Georgia, where one year a fulsomely endowed young woman wearing a badge made out to "Mrs. Raymond Floyd" and precious little else was escorted off the hallowed Augusta National grounds by a Pinkerton guard, for creating a public distraction or something. The next day, a different young woman, wearing the same badge and virtually the same outfit, also was escorted out the front gate.

"If there's anything better than women," Floyd said to me a few years ago in the remnants of a North Carolina drawl, "I don't know what it is. I like women and partying and I'm not ashamed of it. It doesn't affect my golf. I have tremendous recovery power, and all I need is six hours sleep. I don't turn into a pumpkin at midnight."

Partying, he explained, was his way of relaxing from the rigors of the tour. Other players went fishing or played cards; he socialized. "I've never been drunk on a golf course," he said, "but I've teed off with some pretty good hangovers."

He could be unexpectedly serious, however. "Nothing would make me happier than to find a girl I could love, so that I'd want nobody else," he said one afternoon in an empty, lonely locker room at Hartford. "We'd have children. That's what life is all about, isn't it? It's difficult to find that kind of girl playing professional golf, but I'm young and I'm going to be looking."

In 1973, with his career foundering through a fourth straight disappointing year and the righteous-at-heart saying "I told you so," Raymond found her: Maria Primoli, a former airline stewardess from Philadelphia, a lovely, vivacious girl with radiant dark eyes and an awakening wit. She immediately inspired Raymond to change his lifestyle 180 degrees, and the inkling is strong that, given a long weekend, she could convince a leopard to change its spots.

"I knew Raymond's reputation from top to bottom," she said. "They called him a swinger, and he was. Somebody had to land him, though, and I was the lucky one. I'd never seen a golf tournament until I met Raymond at the Palm Bay Club in Miami. Until then I thought a country club was just a place where you went to have dinner."

Nowadays Raymond would rather eat dinner at home with his wife and two young sons, Raymond Jr. and Robert, than go out. His domestication must be seen to be believed. Early to bed and early to rise, relatively speaking. Even jogging and a trimmer physique at 200 pounds. Wrestling with the kids. Hushed exchanges of sweet somethings with Maria.

"I'm glad I waited as long as I did to get married," he says. "Before, I wouldn't have understood what a family means, what a woman like Maria can do for a man. Besides, I don't have anything in the back of my mind that I wish I'd done when I was single. I did it all. I'm not proud of it, but that's the way it was, and if it hadn't been that way I wouldn't treasure so much what I have now."

Bruce Lietzke flew to a tournament with Floyd and his family last year and saw a side of Raymond that few know. "His kids were crawling all over him and crying and all the normal stuff," says Lietzke. "One wanted to go to the bathroom, the other wanted a glass of water. Raymond never got upset. He was patient with them the entire trip. He's a dedicated family man, and that dedication and patience must have carried over to his golf."

Says Tom Weiskopf, "Raymond and I used to run around together when we were single, and I know the transformation he's undergone. He's so engrossed in his family it's almost sappy. He skipped the West Coast swing two years ago because his wife was going to have a baby. A changed lifestyle and an improved swing have made him a new man.

"His swing isn't as flat as it used to be—he's taking the club back a lot better. He's happy and he's capable of playing some fantastic golf. Shooting 17 under par to tie Jack Nicklaus' Masters record in 1976 was one of the greatest feats this game has seen. The course is longer and tougher than when Jack set the record. There are so many places you can get trapped. To keep playing aggressively the way Raymond did was just unbelievable."

Nicklaus made three eagles in the course of the week in '76—and finished 11 shots behind Floyd. "I really didn't expect to see the record tied," Jack said in a tone of voice midway between surprised and shell-shocked. Muttered Larry Ziegler, who fired and fell back the last day, "The last time I had this much fun was during a root-canal operation."

Floyd ripped off rounds of 65-66-70-70 to make the rolling green course blush with embarrassment. A great front runner, he set tournament records at the 36- and 54-hole poles and wound up eight shots ahead of his closest pursuer, Ben Crenshaw, while nearly lapping the field.

When he's hot, Floyd is a four-alarm fire. If he gets a bird in hand, he wants the two in the bush. "I'm aggressive by nature," he says. "I try to birdie every hole. If I don't play that way, I don't make birdies, and if you don't make birdies, you don't win. I charge everything on the greens."

At the '76 Masters, his game was flawless. He drove the ball so far a Southern wit exclaimed, "The only reason it came down is it got tired." He worked his shots from left to right or from right to left at will. His fairway woods—probably the best part of his game — were deadly, particularly the new 5-wood he was carrying in place of a 1-iron. He used it for long approach shots from the hilly Augusta lies, and it was largely responsible for his going 14 under par on the par-5 holes, another tournament record.

When he putted, from near or far, the ball was attracted to the hole as if by a hidden magnet. "People don't appreciate that Raymond consistently is one of the best putters on the tour," says Butch Baird, his friend who lives only a few miles from Floyd in Miami. "He's a big man, but he has a sensitive touch. He's just a good all-round athlete." Ken Still tells the story of going to .a baseball game with Floyd on a hot, muggy night in Cleveland and Floyd snagging one mosquito after another with quick, one-handed moves.

"It's nice to go back to work on your game and have it pay off like this," Floyd said after the Masters victory turned his career around. "The game was easy for me as a kid, and I had to play a while to find out how hard it is."

Floyd was born at Fort Bragg in North Carolina to a career Army man and his wife who have since divorced. "I respect my folks for staying together until my sister and I were raised," he says. (His sister Marlene, a former United Airlines stewardess, was named *Golf Digest's* Most Beautiful Golfer in 1964, and now plays the LPGA tour, with modest success.) "I knew for a long time our parents didn't get along, but they sacrificed for us. I was . deprived of nothing within reason as a child. Dad always bought me the very best sports equipment."

L. B. Floyd ran a driving range on the side before he retired from the service (he now owns a fine public course near Fayetteville, N.C.), and started Ray in golf when he was 5. By the time he was 7, Ray was hitting the ball as far as some men and was hurting his father's range business. "When he'd start hitting, everybody else would stop and watch him—we didn't sell as many buckets," the elder Floyd recalls.

"I never had any trouble with Raymond. He was quiet and easy-going. He won the PGA on my 49th birthday and it was a terrific present."

In high school Ray played quarterback on the football team and pitched for the baseball team, but, unusually, his young body was developing faster than its bone structure, and a doctor ordered him to give up sports. He quit playing football and baseball, and golf's gain may have been baseball's loss. Two years later, after his senior year in high school, the Cleveland

Indians gave him a chance to sign a bonus contract, even though he hadn't thrown for two years, but by then he was committed to golf.

At the age of 17, he won the International Jaycee Junior Championship and became serious about the game for the first time. "He got the first golf scholarship in the history of the University of North Carolina," says his father, "but he left school after three months. Broke my heart."

Following an 18-month stint in the Army, Raymond joined the tour in 1963. He was sponsored by his father and nine other North Carolina businessmen. His early record was atrocious; he failed to make money in his first 10 tournaments, missing the cut in nine.

But in his 11th event, the St. Petersburg Open, he finished first — at age 20, the youngest man to win a PGA tournament since the 1920's. He would — it was roundly predicted — be a future great. By taking pills daily for seven years he had beaten his teenage ailment. However, he did not win again until the St. Paul Open in 1965, and then went winless in 1966, 1967 and 1968.

Going into the 1969 season, the consensus was that Floyd had won too fast and had been adversely influenced by his first roommate, Doug Sanders, and Sanders' carousing buddy, Al Besselink. He was dissipating, it was said, the talent that could have been making him the stellar player of his generation. "That's crap," Floyd says. "I was fortunate to win as soon as I did. There weren't nearly as many good players then. It wasn't until

three years later that I felt I could compete against anybody. I may have been influenced by Sanders and Besselink at first, but I got away from them when I realized that was the wrong place to be."

The second-guessing abated when Floyd won at Jacksonville in 1969, but then after the third round at the Colonial in Fort Worth he reportedly flew to Houston, did not make it back in time to tee off for the final round and defaulted. The rumor mill cranked up again.

Floyd apparently had gone to Houston to see his beloved Chicago Cubbies play the Astros. He, along with touring pro Ken Still, is a devoted Cub fan and has been known to work out with the team, wearing No. 6. (In spring training one year an elderly woman was watching the Cub pitchers — Floyd among them — running across the outfield and remarked: "Who's that fat No. 6? He'll never make the major leagues!")

But at the American Golf Classic in July of 1969, Floyd won again, shooting an unprecedented four rounds under par on the tough Firestone Country Club course to beat Ken Venturi's five-year-old record by seven shots. Tournament officials were less than enchanted when, they say, Floyd was asked to leave a couple of local bars for being loud and when, later, he had the presentation ceremony shortened so he could catch a plane to meet "an important business commitment." A syndicated gossip columnist reported the next day that the "business commitment" was a lively local party. (Floyd says he

missed his plane and had to stay over.)

Floyd, who plays difficult courses at least as well as he plays easy ones, then won the PGA over the arduous National Cash Register course in Dayton, under a threat of disruptions by civil-rights demonstrators. "I've had a couple of police escorts before," he cracked, "but never on a golf course."

He said an improved swing tempo was the crucial factor in his revival. "I was giving a clinic in Pennsylvania that summer and talking about the importance of rhythm, and suddenly it dawned on me that this was my own trouble. I was really burning it from the top. I have a fast tempo, but within that I have my own slow and fast extremes, and I was too fast."

Floyd's father, his only teacher until Jack Grout, who tutors Jack Nicklaus, began working with him in recent years, says today: "He has slowed his backswing tremendously since he came on the tour, and that gives him a chance to work his feet and shift his weight. He can use his lower body swinging down into the ball. He always took the club back so fast because he took it back with his hands and arms. Now he takes it back with the left side of his body working as a unit. He realizes now that you have to use your lower body on

"Oy vay!" Floyd seems to be saying, but in reality he's shielding his eyes from the sun en route to the 1976 Masters title. He tied the Masters record of 271.

the downswing regardless of your strength."

More importantly, Floyd realizes now that he has responsibilities that go beyond golf. "Before, when I played badly I didn't hurt anybody but myself, and that didn't seem to make much difference to me," he says. "I probably took four years off my golf career by living it up so much. But now when I play bad, other people, who are depending on me, get hurt, and that's something entirely different.

"I've mellowed, I guess. It's only recently that I've begun to enjoy golf. The game's finally fun to me. It's part maturity and part hard work."

The game has been changing as he has been changing, Floyd says. "When I broke in 15 years ago, probably only 50 guys were capable of winning on the tour. Now there are 250 players out here who could win next week. All the young players are taught to make a big swing and drive the ball 300 yards, and it's much more an aggressive power game today. Everybody's trying to get birdies all the time, and you can't sit back and play cautiously, not even if you're Jack Nicklaus. The young players never stop going for the flag. They're conditioned to think that no recovery shot is impossible.

"Tougher competition and tougher courses have done that. Once, if you had a hard bunker shot, you said to yourself, 'Well, I've bogeyed this one.' Now you have to gamble on inventing a shot to get close to the hole, because if you don't, you won't win much money. Every player I know on the tour has im-

proved his bunker play in the last 10 years, out of necessity.

"We're playing more testing courses every year—Muirfield Village, Butler National, Sawgrass," he elaborates. "We play a dozen layouts a year that look like U.S. Open courses. Pinehurst No. 2 used to be the great monster course on the tour. Now it's just another course — Hale Irwin shot 20 under par there in 1977. Every time I return to an old course, they've pushed the tees back into somebody's front yard to lengthen it. But if they didn't, we'd be busting records every week.

"I like tougher courses myself, particularly if they put a premium on finesse shots as well as power. I think one reason I'm playing better is that we're on more tough courses. Trouble shots, finesse shots that make you use your brain—that's the pleasure of the game to me. Creating shots is what it's all about."

If Floyd sounds suspiciously like an elder statesman at the age of 35, it's yet another aspect of his lifestyle transplant. He has gone in the last few years, would you believe, from a chaser of women to a leader of men. He recently concluded a two-year term as a player director and the treasurer of the 10-man Tournament Policy Board, the tour's governing group. He impressed the business leaders who serve on the board with his seriousness and contributions. "Frankly, I was surprised," says one. "I'd always heard he was a playboy. But he worked hard to represent the players and the tour the best he could."

Says the former "Pretty Boy"

Floyd, "When your fellow man elects you to an office like that, it shows a lot of confidence that I wanted to justify. I was very involved. I think it was a pivotal term for the board, particularly where the player representatives were concerned. In the past you got on the board more through the buddy system than anything else — one guy went off and his buddy went on. Now it's more of a democratic process.

"I did my homework and tried to stay in touch with all the different groups of players, from the rookies to the superstars. I stayed around the locker room late and listened when somebody had a complaint or suggestion, and I tried to get players out to dinner to find out what they thought about the way the tour was running. I tried to get them to come to the meetings. Most people want to bitch, but they don't want to come to a meeting and sincerely try to get something accomplished. In some cases I succeeded.

"Yes, I'm motivated differently now. My feeling is that I've been out here 15 years and done very well for myself, and now I'm in a position to give something back to the game. I didn't always think this way, and I hope I can convince some of the other fellows, who think too much about themselves and not enough about the big picture, to help our tour.

"I don't enter many foreign tournaments or do many exhibitions, because I feel I should use that time to play the American tour as much as possible. That's what made me, so why not help our tour while I still can? That's why I was glad to serve on the policy board.

"That board holds the future of the tour in its hands, because it sets policy. In our sport, the commissioner's job is not really to set policy —it's to carry out policy. I think the roles had been reversed to some extent, but that's changed. The board can't be just a rubber stamp for the commissioner. We wanted it known, when he was moving to end the tour earlier in the year, for instance, that just because he's the commissioner he can't do as he pleases. I think he's doing a great job, but I also think the board needed and got a stronger voice.

"The players are learning that we have a crucial responsibility. Golf is a big business. We have to be more aware of our fans and sell our talent and personalities. I tried to help that learning process along, and I found it very educational myself. Being on the board took a lot of time—I was on the phone at all hours and had to answer a lot of correspondence — but it was worth it. It was a very rewarding experience.

"My wife was a big help. She's a businesswoman herself — people think she was just a stewardess, but she's an owner of two fashion and design schools, the Bauder Fashion Colleges in Atlanta and Miami, and she's a bright, organized person. She doesn't like me to talk about her, but I have to say she's changed my life."

It goes without saying, actually. There is no need for a brightly lit marquee screaming "WELCOME HOME, RAY FLOYD." The new Ray Floyd is home.

Raymond Floyd, once known as a playboy, is a family man now. Above, Raymond and his wife Maria take their two children, Raymond Jr. and Robert, on a Biscayne Bay cruise in a boat owned by Carling Dinkler. Dinkler also owns the Palm Bay Club in Miami where the Floyds live, at right. On opposite page, Maria prepares a meal, while Raymond Jr. watches and Raymond holds Robert. Below, the family relaxes in front of a waterfall at the Palm Bay Club. The baseball picture demonstrates Raymond's long-standing fierce devotion to the Chicago Cubs — with him is pitcher Ken Holtzman. Raymond still has a Cubs' locker.

BOB TOSKI: Ray Floyd is an excellent fairway woods player, and anybody who is an excellent fairway woods player has learned to play within himself. You have to have good tempo to hit the fairway woods as well as Raymond Floyd does—you cannot rush the swing.

Ray's leg action sets him apart from the other top players we're studying. His leg action is a little different, as we will see.

First, though, I like his address position. His arms are hanging well, almost vertically downward from his shoulders, and he looks comfortable.

But on his takeaway he pushes the club straight back from the ball farther than most good players. His club comes straight back and then rather abruptly up.

His left knee moves more quickly in the backswing than I would have expected—it rolls toward the right knee sooner. His quick left-knee movement would be fine except that Ray's right knee begins to straighten early in the backswing, and that makes him work harder than he should. He gets off his left side nicely, but his right side — his right leg — doesn't resist as firmly as it should. The right leg straight-

ens and keeps him from getting behind the ball at the top of the swing as well as some of the other strong players. He would be better off if he retained the flex in his right knee that he had at address.

As his backswing progresses, his body controls his arms more than his arms control his body. I would rather see the arms pacing the swing, because you get a freer, more relaxed flow. Ray almost turns first and swings second.

Even so, he makes a big, full backswing—by the time he reaches the top he has coiled his upper body tremendously. That shows he possesses fine physical flexibility, and also that he took his time on his backswing and allowed his body to wind up this completely. The club has dropped below horizontal, which I wouldn't recommend for most players, but Ray is big enough and strong enough to keep it under control. He hasn't "lost" the club with his left hand.

With his right leg straightened at the top of his swing, Ray is prone to throw the club down with his hands and lose power and direction.

He recovers rather well in this swing because he has a good, firm

left-wrist position at the top and a good, strong left-arm movement starting down. If he didn't move so well with the left arm, he would be in trouble due to his right leg staying that straight.

In Ray's swing, the club lowers rapidly from the top, which indicates that his legs aren't driving toward the target as well as they could be. He doesn't drive from his right leg to his left leg as quickly as other leading players, in large measure because the right leg got too straight earlier.

Ray has said that when he's playing poorly he doesn't give his legs time to work on the downswing, and that's what we see here to some extent. He's changing directions at the top mainly with his arms and hands. Ideally, his hands would remain passive starting down. Then his legs could drive forward and support his arm swing coming down into the ball.

In this respect, Ray's problem—when it is one—is similar to the one I see every day in average golfers. They pressure the club with the hands at the start of the downswing and "hit from the top." They get in too big a hurry to use the hands.

Unlike weekend golfers, Ray is

very strong and agile, and when he gets out of position during his swing he has the athletic ability to make an adjustment and bring the club back to the ball squarely. Most of us don't have that kind of strength and agility. His left arm works hard in this swing to make up for the negative tendencies we've noted. The left arm is in command of the downswing, and he retains the angle between the left forearm and the shaft of the club until he's more than halfway down. Then he releases the angle to apply his power where he needs it—in the hitting area.

This is a big, strong swing that is "on" much more often than it is "off." When it lets Ray down now and then, I think you can see why: The right leg straightens on the backswing, and he then is prone to throw the club from the top with his hands. But he has great athletic ability, and he does a lot more things right than wrong.

ARNOLD PALMER

To place a President of the United States in proper historical perspective might take several generations, but to evaluate the impact of Arnold Palmer on golf we need not wait. He has meant more to the game than anyone, ever, in virtually every conceivable way. His vibrant personality, aided by the world-shrinking capabilities of television, has made him the best-known American athlete of this or any other age, and probably the most venerated.

He still draws bigger crowds on the practice putting green than other top professionals attract on the course. He is still cheered loudly by hordes of fans ranging from 8 to 80 when he so much as hitches up his slacks with characteristic Palmer flair: "Go get 'em, Arnie!"

Unfortunately, Arnie has not been going and getting them as in days of yore, but his popularity has scarcely waned.

A few years ago a man who managed tour events for a living told me that having Arnold Palmer in a tournament could be worth 20,000 spectators. I'm sure that figure has shrunk somewhat, but Palmer is still a major attraction, particularly in the smaller tournaments. To some extent the fans empathize with his recent travails as they always have empathized with his bold trouble shots; they can see themselves in Palmer.

"Galleries now flock to him because they don't know how much longer they'll have the chance," says a tournament director. "You see a broader mix following him, with a lot of young people who never saw him before. His crowds are more hopeful than uproarious with anticipation now—they sense that he won't make one of his famous charges, but they know he's still capable of putting together a stretch of exciting shot-making."

Palmer's place in the record books is secure. He is the winner of 61 PGA Tour events and eight major championships (he personally

rejuvenated the venerable British Open when it was foundering for lack of American support). He is the first to have won a million dollars playing the game, and he did it with a slashing, hard-charging style that endeared him to every weekend golfer who's been stymied behind a bush on the last hole with a dollar nassau bet at stake.

Palmer may well have lost as many tournaments as he's won with his let-it-all-hang-out finishes, but it is his dramatic successes that we remember. In 1960, most memorably, he trailed Mike Souchak by seven strokes through 54 holes of the U.S. Open at Cherry Hills in Denver. Then, after a lunch break that separated the last two rounds, he drove the 346-yard first hole to start the final 18, went on to hang up a scorching 65 and won the tournament to establish himself as the game's dominant figure.

He had the personality for the role. He has always been handsome in a rugged sort of way, and he has always thrived on public attention. He can look into a gallery of thousands, smile his infectious smile and give every single fan the impression that he or she is being singularly favored.

He has never been known to refuse an autograph, snarl at an overbearing drunk or duck a press interview. "Arnold," says a man who has known him since his rookie year, "suffers fools more gladly than any other man in sport. That's a big reason he's a legend

Even superstars feel the pain when they miss birdie putts in the U.S. Open.

in his own time."

It is easy to forget that legends had to start somewhere. The legend of Arnold Palmer started at the Masters Tournament in Georgia, in the late 1950's.

Palmer's image as a "charger," a player who shoots at the pin no matter where it's positioned, was born there. So was "Arnie's Army" of dedicated fans, not coincidentally.

The course suited his game immediately. He says, "Augusta National is a difficult course, but if you hit the shots, you can birdie any hole. I think that helps a player like me. The course gives the bold player an advantage and can swallow up the cautious player. If you start playing safe for pars here you're liable to come up with a fast string of bogeys."

The aggressive Palmer has won the Masters four times, a total surpassed only by Jack Nicklaus. His fame began to grow in the '58 Masters, when he first won.

Then during his victory in 1960, a young worker on a scoreboard out on the course put up a sign hailing the coming of Arnie and his army of followers. A local sports writer used the slogan "Arnie's Army" the next day and it stuck. Palmer caught and passed Ken Venturi in 1960, birdieing the tough last two holes as Venturi watched dejectedly on television in the clubhouse. That started the talk about his ability to come from behind.

Palmer's best Masters and his best major championship came in 1964. He played with unapproachable consistency to shoot 69, 68, 69 and 70 and win by six strokes.

That was Palmer's last victory in a major championship. There has been considerable speculation in recent years over whether he should retire. What does he think?

"Every time I shoot 75, people want to know when I'm going to quit," he says with a rueful smile. "I was getting that question 10 years ago.

"Sure, it's frustrating when you can't make things happen you're trying to. All areas of my game are reasonably good. I'm driving better than ever, and my putting is OK. I just lack a touch of concentration, of consistency. I'll have a mental letdown on a shot and it'll cost me severely. It might be a drive or a chip. There's no pattern to it.

"I don't think I'll ever really retire. A baseball or football player might retire, but a golfer never does, even if he says he will. He keeps playing. Even Byron Nelson, who pretty much retired in his prime, came back and played some tournaments. I'd trim my schedule—but I'm not ready to do that yet. I love the game as much as ever. The other day I played at the club at home with three members—in the rain—and had a terrific time.

"What makes me confident I can come back? I guess the same thing that made me think I could get it going when I started. The answer is to work harder."

Many close followers of golf doubt that the answer is that simple. They are afraid that Palmer's age (approaching 50) and swing (forceful) are taking an inevitable toll. They are embarrassed for him when he struggles to break 80.

77

While it is a tribute to Palmer's immense popularity that no one publicly calls for his retirement, there are those connected with the tour who privately speak of him as they might speak of a venerable race horse that should be put out to pasture. They believe that if his candle is not out, as Shakespeare put it, it definitely is flickering low.

Says one of Palmer's contemporaries, "He should stop now, before he ruins his image. There's nothing worse in any sport than an athlete who keeps playing past his prime."

Rumors abound that an aging Palmer is troubled by physical infirmities. Most frequently you hear that his hip bothers him, or that he has an inner-ear condition that affects his balance.

The truth is that he has had no pain in the once bothersome hip for several years, and his balance is fine except when he occasionally swings too hard. He *is* slightly hard of hearing, as his late father Deacon was, but that could be an advantage in competitive golf.

Palmer contends that his swing is unimpaired. More than one expert sees unwelcome changes in his action, however. "It's always been a swing that requires greater physical stress than most," says a leading teacher. "For instance, you have to be awfully strong to have your left wrist bowed at the top of the swing and hold that position through impact. With the face of the club closed at the top, you need great leg drive through the ball to avoid a terrible hook. I see less leg drive and more spinning out in Arnold's swing now. At the Masters I saw him hook a ball across two fairways."

It is unlikely that Palmer could change his swing at this stage of his career. He possibly could regain strength and flexibility through an advanced exercise program.

Sam Snead still swings magnificently—but is blessed with a loose-jointed body and a naturally smooth swing. Sam, of course, will be winning money when he is 104.

"It would be wonderful if Arnold eventually could get into Sam's position, where he isn't expected to win but comes out on the tour almost to play exhibitions," says Tom Place, the tour press secretary. "Nobody thinks of Sam as an old warrior looking for one last kill."

Unfortunately, Palmer is 15 or 20 years away from being able to think about moving gracefully into the kind of unique role that Snead enjoys.

When I asked his peers what they thought Palmer should do, the prevalent reply was that he should cut down his schedule. Jack Nicklaus, Palmer's long-time friendly rival, gave a thoughtful answer.

"Sooner or later, what Arnold is going through happens to every person in every walk of life," Nicklaus said. "He's done so much for the game, nobody likes to see him suffer. The unfortunate part is that he is quite capable of winning—but he doesn't know it. I think it could be better if he spotted himself to play six or seven times a year. It

Palmer in recent years has tried both glasses and contact lenses in the unwavering hope of winning another major championship.

would be a real happening every time he played. Ben Hogan did that.

"But the other side of it is that Arnold loves to play, to compete. If he wants to play, more power to him. We talk about golf being the game of a lifetime, and this is the game of his life. If he's happy playing, then that's what he should do."

Says another leading pro, "If Arnold asked me what he ought to do, I'd tell him to play six to 10 favorite tournaments, in places where he's won, where he has a lot of friends, where he likes the courses. Places where he has every chance to do well, and if he catches a hot putting week he might win. Places like Palm Springs. I'd tell him to hold to that schedule."

Palmer will play about 25 tournaments a year counting foreign trips. He never has reduced his schedule appreciably—in 1966 he played 27 tournaments. He often has said he plans to cut back, but he never does. Partly he fears he would lose his competitive edge, partly he usually cannot say no to a tournament sponsor who calls to say he needs him.

Several insiders wish Palmer had been offered the tour commissioner's job when Joe Dey stepped down and turned the office over to Deane Beman, then a tour player, in 1974.

"Arnold would be a fine commissioner," says one, "because he knows golf and is a decent man who has business experience. And he would be able to go on being Arnold Palmer."

The consensus today is that Beman is doing a good job and can keep the commissionership as long as he wants it, which would seem to close off that possibility to Palmer.

Whatever he does whenever his playing career ends, Palmer is assured of being a rich man for the rest of his life. He could keep busy running his various businesses, but probably won't. He likes to play golf too much and is too restless.

A future possibility would be to play exhibitions around the world, as Walter Hagen did in his later years. Palmer then would be playing golf, would be staying in the public eye and would be enhancing his business interests.

A man close to Palmer, a supposedly unimpeachable source, says Palmer is seriously considering running for governor or senator in his home state of Pennsylvania. "It appeals to him in terms of image," says the man. "It wouldn't be a step down from golf. But I hope he doesn't do it. I can't imagine him in front of a hostile press conference."

It also is difficult to imagine the PGA tour without Arnold Palmer. Think about it. We frequently hear about a young player who is billed as "the next Arnold Palmer." There will be no next Arnold Palmer. There will be another Hubert Green or another Johnny Miller, perhaps, but there will never be another Arnold Palmer. He brought his irresistible magnetism to the sport just as television and President Eisenhower helped launch the golf boom. He became the first golfer to expand the appeal of the tour to the bleacher fans.

Should he retire? I like an answer I got from Larry Eldridge, the sports editor of The Christian Science Monitor. "Who are we to tell him

what to do?" Eldridge said. "How many of us would retire? I don't buy the idea that he's tarnishing his image by continuing to play. Posterity won't care. Babe Ruth wound up his career with a couple of awful seasons, but his place in history is secure." So is Arnold Palmer's. He has earned the right to decide for himself when to quit.

People who ought to know say that Palmer's businesses are assured of continued success whatever he does on the course. Listen to a vice president of the Rockwell Manufacturing Company, for whom Palmer endorses a line of power tools: "He's beyond having to win. As far as many people are concerned, he will always be the champ." Agrees Mark McCormack, his manager: "We feel Arnold has reached the point where his golf successes aren't terribly important to his enterprises anymore. He is a millionaire several times over."

With his life in a transitional period, I asked Palmer to reflect on his unique career and the qualities that have made him one of the most famous athletes of all time.

We talked intensively in an interview that began behind the double doors of his paneled office next to his home in Youngstown after he spent from 7:30 to 9:30 a.m. answering mail. It continued through the day while an ever-restless Palmer, uncomfortable at a desk, moved to the golf club he had purchased across the street and then to his workshop and club storage area. He took an hour out to film recruiting commercials for the

Coast Guard. Twice McCormack called to talk business for 30 minutes.

On a warm day, he wore a deep-necked white golf shirt, subtly checked red slacks and white loafers with no socks. The familiar voice was nasally resonant, and he proved unusually voluble.

SEITZ: What do you think it would take to be another Arnold Palmer? What qualities?

PALMER: "I never thought about what it would take to be the *original* Arnold Palmer. I just knew what my goals and desires were, and tried to work toward them. I've always been an aggressive, ambitious golfer. I had to be—when I started I didn't have much money. I've always enjoyed being around people. I wouldn't know how to start over, and you couldn't build my personality into someone else. You couldn't make a man who doesn't enjoy being with people *like* people. If you're not genuine, people sense that."

SEITZ: You had been in the service and worked as a manufacturer's representative before you turned pro at 25.

PALMER: "Yes, and I think it helped me, starting later. A young amateur plays against the pros once or twice and does pretty well, and he thinks it's an easy way to make a living. Well, there's pain and anguish that you find out about only by traveling the tour. I played in the Wilmington Open in North Carolina when I was a junior in college, I think it was, and did well. I shot 65 the first round and played like Lanny Wadkins did at the

82

Heritage Classic one year, and I thought I was pretty hot stuff, as he thought he was. But I hesitated to turn pro. I didn't have the financial means, and I wasn't sure I was prepared psychologically, so I stayed away. And very fortunately so, because it gave me time to decide just what I wanted to do. When I did turn pro, it was tough. I made it because I had matured enough to know what I was getting into."

SEITZ: How did the added maturity help?

PALMER: "We're talking about a young man who goes through high school as a star golfer and then is a star golfer in college, and in the summers he plays in big amateur tournaments where the surroundings are as nice as they can be. The country clubs are the best and the courses are all of a certain kind, very well manicured. He has status — everyone recognizes him and is attentive to him. He's staying in fine private homes with friendly people, and being entertained royally — because he's a big amateur champion.

"He turns professional, and suddenly he's only one of 400 guys who travel the country trying to earn a living at golf, and hitting the ball pretty well. He's no longer famous. Golf becomes a working life instead of a game. He's spending hours on practice, and being ignored because he hasn't proved anything yet in this league. He's staying in a motel that isn't the best, and maybe eating in cafeterias. At night he sits in his room or goes to the movies, but he has a lot of time to wonder. He may have to drive hundreds of miles by himself, get to the next tournament site, and tee up to try to qualify on Monday. You think at first it will be great to travel, but there's no time for sightseeing.

"What he thought would be a highly glamorous way of living isn't so glamorous. If he has ability, practices hard, doesn't let the pressure bother him, and understands the things I'm talking about, he'll make it. But it's a terrible adjustment."

SEITZ: Was money as big a lure to turn professional for you as it seems to be today?

PALMER: "The money is greater in every way. The first few years I played the tour, the winners' checks were $1,500 and $2,000. That's a long way from $50,000, but it wasn't bad. I think working into the bigger money the way I did — winning $3,000 and $6,000 and then $10,000 and $15,000 and $20,000 — was good for me. It happened gradually, and I was able to learn to handle the money. I grew up with the purses. But my main ambition was not simply to make money — I wanted to play golf well."

SEITZ: Was there ever any doubt in your mind that you would reach the top?

PALMER: "I was always too busy trying hard to think much about failing, but in those early days on the tour I was looking around at golf courses and learning about the superintendent's job and the pro's job—in case I needed something to fall back on. I knew I wanted to be around a golf course. I grew up on one, and I always enjoyed it, working or playing. It's a healthy way

to go. I knew I couldn't work indoors. In the service I spent a great deal of time in an office, and that wasn't for me. Then when I was national amateur champion in 1954, I had a vague hope of becoming a good businessman and a top amateur golfer, too, playing in all the big amateur and open events. Then I decided I wanted to try the tour."

SEITZ: And yet today you have dozens of commercial involvements. How do you make an important business decision?

PALMER: "If I control the matter, I make it myself. I may discuss it with Doc Giffin and my assistants here. If it's a legal decision, I go to Mark McCormack's office in Cleveland. If it's a tax decision, I go to my attorneys. The purchase of the Latrobe Country Club across the way was a deal I handled myself, because I was familiar with the circumstances. That deal wasn't made to show a big profit. I wanted to be sure I stayed close to the club, because it's always meant a great deal to me."

In celebrating its 25th anniversary a few years ago, *Golf Digest* named a Man of the Silver Era. The choice was easy: Arnold Daniel Palmer of Latrobe, Pennsylvania. His acceptance speech said much about the man and why he deserved the honor:

"I'm flattered for a lot of reasons," he began. "I'm thrilled by the honor *Golf Digest* has bestowed on me. I think back to my boyhood days at the Latrobe Country Club. My father working on the tractor, cutting fairways, and me busting for a chance to get on that tractor and help him.

"I can't tell you how much I appreciate golf. It's been my life. They talk about what I have done for the game ... all I can say to you is, what the game has done for me! Whatever I've given the game isn't enough. You can't give enough to a game like golf.

"I'd like to get this message across to people just coming into golf, that whatever you're doing, cutting the fairways at Latrobe Country Club, or owning Latrobe Country Club, golf has so much to offer that you can never give it enough. My contributions are insignificant. When you honor me, you honor golf, not me."

The honors have only begun to descend on Arnold Palmer.

Arnold and friends line up a putt on the practice green at the Walt Disney Classic in Florida.

A smiling Arnold at his desk at home and, at right, with his family: Peggy, wife Winnie and Amy, now Mrs. Roy Saunders. Below, Arnold discusses club design in his workshop with a group of Xerox executives during a corporate outing in Latrobe, Pa. On opposite page, he accepts his "Man of the Silver Era" award commemorating the 25th anniversary of *Golf Digest* magazine. "Whatever I've given golf is insignificant," Palmer said, with typical modesty. "When you honor me, you honor golf, not me."

Arnold Palmer has long been absorbed in flying. Above, on a trip to England, a friend asked him if he would like to take an antique plane up for a spin. Arnold obliged, looking like a World War I pilot. At right, he checks the controls of his own Cessna Citation jet and poses proudly with the aircraft.

BOB TOSKI: What has made Palmer a great player is his ability to get the ball in the hole, plus he's very strong. His inside-out golf swing is largely a result of his posture.

He sets up farther from the ball than most players do. He reaches for the ball, and the more he reaches, the more he's going to take the club around his body. The path of the swing is going to be more around and flat and not so upright.

In his takeaway, the clubface will not move along the target line as far as that of Nicklaus, for example.

It moves inside earlier.

I think a lot of this has to do with the influence of Arnold's late father, a club professional who taught him to play. Arnold was taught to make a big body turn, and so he makes a quicker shoulder turn and a quicker hip turn than most players. Palmer swings to the top with his right leg nearly straight, because anytime the bigger muscles turn as fast as his do, the right leg cannot resist as easily and has to straighten. That makes him work harder to keep his swing on track.

I would much prefer to see Palmer's arms controlling the path of the swing and the shoulders serving as nothing but what I call carriers—the shoulders are nothing but a base on which the arms travel. The shoulders respond to the arms, ideally. If my arms swing and my shoulders carry the momentum of my arms, then I have the chance to move my arms wherever I want to. But if my arms instead are responsive to my shoulders, I have very little choice where my arms go.

When Arnold takes the club that far inside on the backswing, his tendency will be to try to move it back out to the target line earlier on the downswing. The club makes a quick reverse loop. In the forward action of his body, the hips and shoulders rotate quicker to the left to allow the force of the swing to move back on line and square the clubface against the ball. Palmer is what I call a twister and turner with a blocking action through the impact area. He blocks with his left hand and arm, using them as a fulcrum through the ball so that the force of the right arm and hand will

not break down the left hand and arm.

His left arm has to work very strongly on the downswing, because he has a straighter left leg coming down than most superstars. Since his left leg cannot support the forward swing, his great left-arm strength is all that's left.

His leg action is entirely too restricted because he sets up with too much weight on his left side—his left leg becomes the support leg for his backswing when his right leg should be. Then when he makes that big shoulder turn, his

right leg straightens. If your body controls your arms, you tend to leave your weight where it was set up. In Arnold's case, that's on his left side. He isn't able to get his weight behind the ball on his backswing as I would prefer, and then he isn't able to shift his weight through the ball on the downswing.

Since Palmer's an in-to-out swinger, he more or less is a hooker of the golf ball. He fears the ball starting left and going left. You can see it in his impact position. He finishes the way he does because he is fearful of the ball going way left. He uses

the strength of his left arm to counteract the turn of his hips which ordinarily would make the clubface pull the ball left. Most players wouldn't have the strength in the left arm to do that.

Arnold never uses his legs as well as he should because when the path of swing moves inside so abruptly, the body subsequently has to turn abruptly left on the downswing to allow the path to come back to the target line. Therefore, he can't move his legs, and if he can't move his legs, he's got to use the upper part of his body.

If Arnold's head position were not as stable as it is through the entire swing, he would not strike the ball as solidly and squarely as he does. His body revolves under and around his head, and his head position stays steady. It doesn't move forward with the force of the blow.

The beautiful part of Arnold Palmer's golf swing is the way his head stays steady and his left arm stabilizes the blow. It takes a lot of effort, but he effectively controls the face of the club through the ball.

JOHNNY MILLER

Johnny Miller is golf's rejoinder to that little girl in the nursery rhyme who had a little curl. When she was good, she was very, very good, but when she was bad, she was horrid and probably could not break 80. At his best, Johnny Miller may be the finest player ever. He can be, in the carefully chosen words of sporting historian Herbert Warren Wind, "almost confoundingly brilliant." But at his worst Miller can disappear from contention with mercurial quickness.

Miller has shot more near-perfect rounds than anyone else active today. When he's hot, he can "run the table" in the vernacular of pool players, pool being one of Miller's several avidly pursued diversions from golf. He came from back in the pack, for example, to run away with the 1973 U.S. Open at Oakmont, shooting a shocking final-round 63 that is the lowest score of all time in our national championship. He hit every green in regulation numbers, did not make a five, and easily could have scored lower.

Monumental though that round is, it practically pales in comparison with what Miller did to start the 1974 tour season. He won the opening three tournaments—the Bing Crosby National Pro-Am, the Phoenix Open and the Tucson Open—and shot par or better in his first 23 rounds! He ultimately finished the year with eight victories and a tour money record, still standing, of more than $353,000!

As comfortable in the desert as a cactus, Miller started the following season nearly as fast, winning at Phoenix by 14 strokes with a 24-under-par total of 260 and at Tucson by nine with a 25-under 263. All eight rounds were in the 60's, and he shot a 61 each week.

But, at the other extreme, Miller can miss cuts by gaping margins, play far below his peak in one major championship after another and just generally disappoint himself and his followers for months on

end. In 1977, unbelievably, he was a distant 48th on the money list, with earnings of only about $61,000, and failed to win a tournament.

Can this be the same Johnny Miller who so often makes a mockery of par? Who, when he's on, perhaps has no equal?

If Miller's sporadic brilliance is confounding, his not-infrequent slumps are even more so. His inconsistency baffles astrologers, graphologists, biorhythmists. He is an enigma wrapped in an enigma, and trying to solve the Mystery of the Erratic Superstar is like opening a set of those practical-joke gift boxes in which the unwrapping of one box only leaves you with a slightly smaller box-within-a-box.

Why is Miller so streaky?

"I think it's in the level of his desire to play," says Rod Funseth, a fellow tour player who lives near Miller in Napa, California, alongside the Silverado Country Club course. "I can pretty much tell how he's going to play by how enthused he is. If he feels like playing, he's liable to have one of those lights-out days. I played with him in Arizona when he was on one of his tears, and I don't think anybody's ever played that well. It was early in the year and he was rested and fired up, and he just about knocked down every flagstick. The amazing thing when he's playing like that is how accurate he is with his distance on iron shots. He's never 20 feet long or short. Even though you know the exact yardages, you still have to visualize the shot and feel the swing before you make it, and he does that better than anybody. I've also played with him when I got the impression he would just as soon have been somewhere else, not playing golf. You have to understand that Johnny genuinely enjoys himself at home. He likes his family and he likes hunting and fishing and he likes driving fast cars and motorcycles and working around the ranch near his home.

"Some people thrive on being in the limelight, but Johnny Miller doesn't. I think Johnny's on the shy side. When his game isn't good, he gets embarrassed and down.

"I've never seen him work very hard at his game. The year he won eight tournaments, he'd take a lot of time off and get completely away from golf, then go back out on tour and pick up where he left off. Now he's 30 years old and finding he can't do that anymore. He used to fly home when a tournament ended on Sunday, not touch a club, then fly to the next tournament on Wednesday. Now it's not working. He's learning he needs a couple of practice rounds, the same as everybody else. He was able to play well before without working hard at it, and now that he can't, it's frustrating for him.

"There could be another factor. Johnny is bigger and stronger than people think—he's no skinny kid. To build up his endurance he's worked on his ranch and lifted weights, and I think he got too strong for golf in certain muscle

Miller's caddie, Andy Martinez, popularized the caddie crouch to block out gallery movement from behind and help his golfer align putts. The rulemakers eventually vetoed the practice.

groups. Some of his muscles are tight, and that isn't good for this game. I'll tell you, I wouldn't want to arm-wrestle him.

"But there's still plenty of greatness left in Johnny. One good round can set him off. His confidence soars and he's unbeatable. He knows what he has to do. At first he didn't care. Then he cared, but he couldn't get his swing going."

Miller's fluctuating motivation long has been suspect among other tour players. One tournament winner says, "He lacks the tenacity and dedication of a Ben Hogan. If he had Hogan's determination, he might never lose." Allowing for a touch of overstatement there, it certainly is true that Miller's attitude has been the reverse of Ben Hogan's work ethic. If Hogan finished fourth in a tournament but felt he was not striking the ball purely enough, he would cancel out of the next two tournaments, go home and do little but beat practice balls for two weeks.

Hogan had an understanding and enduring wife and no children. Miller, by contrast, is torn between his allegiance to home—because, in his view, there's no place like it for being with your wife and kids— and the tour, which makes him wealthy and gives him a chance to fulfill his foremost talent in the sport he loves. So far he has been unable to strike the proper balance, in his own mind, between the two pulls. And that has to confuse and perturb him although he is careful not to let any inner turmoil show.

"My attitude toward life isn't affected too much by what happens on tour," Miller says matter-of-

factly, as he carries his own bag across another in a long gray line of locker rooms. "If I'm playing well, it's nice. If I'm not, the world isn't going to stop turning. I'm constantly amazed at all the importance people attach to a game. I guess a lot of people would really relish the adulation I've received. I'm sure Arnold Palmer would love it. He'd be going out to the driving range after a good round so people could crowd around him and he could bask in it. All that attention makes him feel important, and he needs it. I think that's fine for Arnold—he's tremendous. But it's not great for me. I can't handle it."

After a decade of intrigued Miller-watching, I reflect on remarks like those with mixed sentiments. I often wonder if "he doth protest too much" when he downplays the significance of the tour—or of the major championships which he hasn't won as often as some other people who speak of them as the be-all and end-all. But I am convinced that Miller is a sincere family man who can live, at peace with himself, without the trappings of fame. His religion—he is a Mormon—is no small influence on his philosophy. "I am a man in the world but not of the world," he says.

I cannot conceive, though, of Miller forsaking the tour at the age of 30 to go off and lead a life of anonymous domesticity on the ranch. The game means more to him than he lets on, and he was committed to starting the 1978 schedule with a blast of rockets.

"I worked on my game more in 1977 than I had since I turned pro," he says. "I got heavy—over 190 pounds—and I ran and lost weight. I got stronger as well as bigger, and that quickened the tempo of my swing. I was lunging on the downswing. I studied pictures of my swing, before and after. I hit a lot of balls. I'm paying the price."

Miller's controlled monotone seldom varies, and his detached expression rarely changes, but when he's excited the words tumble out in an inadvertent rush that gives away fast-running undercurrents of emotion. "It was a crazy year," he says of 1977, "but there comes a time when you have to realize that no job is easy. I'm not going to rebuild my game completely—I'm patient and my play goes in cycles —but you have to work at it. I wasn't willing to do that a while back, but my attitude has changed. It all goes back to motivation. Nicklaus said he went through the same adjustment when he was about my age. The last two years I lost motivation. I had a bad shoulder and wrist for a while, but they didn't hamper me as much as my attitude did.

"This slump didn't start in 1977— it started in 1976. I won the British Open and made pretty good money in the U.S. in '76, but I thought I had a poor year. I think after those good years in '74 and '75 I just got burned out. You have to realize I've been playing golf intensively for over 20 years—that's a lot of shots. I even thought about quitting. But a couple of weeks off the tour and I'm chomping to get back. Sometimes we have to be shaken to realize how good we have it. It's like a guy playing the slot machines. When he's winning, it's so easy he gets the idea he can keep winning even if he doesn't put any money in the machines. Life doesn't work that way."

A few experts who have watched Miller's game develop allege that he sometimes is too self-reliant when it comes to repairing his swing. He's knowledgeable about the golf swing, they concede, but his is a big, bravura action that leaves a good deal of room for error, and lately it seems to have lost a measure of the exquisite balance on which it is heavily dependent. "He also tends to reduce his troubles to putting," says a member of the tour field staff. "He putts those flat greens in Arizona well to start the year, then when he can't maintain that pace, he thinks his putting is letting him down more than it really is."

When Miller wants help with his game, he still goes to John Geertsen, the longtime teaching professional at the San Francisco Golf Club who has been tutoring him for 23 years, since Miller was 7. Miller considers him a second father. Geertsen recalls, "I met him not long after tragedy struck his family and more or less brought us together. His older brother fell off the rocks fishing in the ocean and drowned. I knew the parents, and not long afterward I saw them at church and inquired about Johnny. It turned out his father had been teaching him golf on a mat in the garage since Johnny was 5. I invited Johnny over to the club and began working with him for 15 minutes to an hour three or four times a week. He already had a pretty good idea of the fundamentals, and

99

he sincerely wanted to learn. He was one of the littlest fellas for his age I've ever seen, but he took a long swing to get distance, and by the time he was 10 he had an excellent swing that basically has stayed with him.

"He's so good with his middle irons today because he practically cut his teeth with a 5-iron and 7-iron. Until he was 10, he always practiced with those two clubs.

"Shortly after he started with me, we began playing a little game that he has carried through with us. I'd always keep one ball in my pocket during a lesson, and at the end of the lesson I'd put that ball down and say, 'John, this is for the U.S. Open. You have to hit that 75-yard sign out there.' He'd bear down—get dead serious—and it's amazing how close he'd come to that sign every time. He still uses variations of that little game to train his mind. Not long ago I was up working with him for a few days, and we went out and played two balls each for 12 holes. All the way around we'd say 'This is for the U.S. Open' or 'This is for the Masters.'

"I think," continues Geertsen, "John decided he wanted to be the greatest golfer in the world shortly after the first time we worked together. His dad, who is a security officer for RCA in San Francisco, talked to him from the onset about being the best, and made sure he worked at what I told him to do. His father sometimes forced him to practice more than he wanted to—he had Johnny at it all the time—but that brought Johnny along, and Johnny never resented it. People who say his father pushed him too hard don't know the relationship between them.

"Whenever Johnny played in a junior tournament in the area, his father and I would try to be there to watch him. He began competing when he was 9, and during the summer months he played a tournament every week. I think the turning point in his career came in the semifinals of the USGA Junior in 1964, in Oregon. John was 1 down through 13 holes. The 14th was a 190-yard par 3, and his opponent hit his tee shot eight feet from the hole. Johnny followed with one of the few hooks he's ever hit, into the trees to the left of the green, but the ball kicked out onto the green, about 20 feet from the hole. He sank the putt for a birdie, the other boy missed his eight-footer, and instead of being 2 down, Johnny was even in the match. He went on to win the match and the tournament and establish himself on the national level.

"It helped John growing up that he was able to play a lot at good courses like San Francisco Golf Club and Olympic, which gave him a junior membership. Those are U.S. Open-type courses where you have to drive straight, hit your irons high and putt fast greens well. I'll never forget following Johnny when he played in the 1966 Open at Olympic. He was only 19 and a sophomore at Brigham Young University, and he'd planned to caddie in the tournament until he qualified for it. I remember him saying he wanted to make some date money so he didn't have to bum it off his dad. The last day, an incident occurred

that shows what a great attitude he has for this game. On the 15th hole, a medium length par 3, he overshot the green and was in that thick, long rough the USGA grows for the Open. His ball was two feet in front of a gallery rope, and the marshals laid down the rope so he could play the shot. But on his backswing, somebody accidentally pulled the rope, and it came up and caught Johnny's club. He hit the ball only six inches. He just walked away from the ball calmly, looked at the shot again—and plopped the ball out of the rough and into the hole for a par! That clinched low amateur for him, and he decided to try to birdie every hole the rest of the way, which was a mistake. He took a couple of bogeys and tied for eighth. But that's one reason Johnny makes low scores—he's not afraid to shoot a really low number like a lot of players are. If he makes three birdies, he doesn't get conservative. He tries to make three more.

"Knowing him as I do," concludes Geertsen, "I think he's worked harder to get where he is than anybody else ever has. Everything he's won in golf, he's earned. You can get to a point, you know, where you have a fine golf swing and can practice too much. Johnny's a great believer in mental practice. He'll sit at home analyzing his game in his head for an hour and do more good than he could by hitting a thousand range balls."

Miller has said much the same thing, which has done absolutely nothing to endear him to other pros. When he was on top, he gave the impression the game was as easy for him as letting his blond hair grow, and players who were struggling cultivated a keen dislike for him. His candor and outward aloofness make him probably the least popular superstar among the tour players.

"I guess some of the things I've said sounded cocky to some people," he says. "You know, the brash kid who hadn't paid his dues. I was 26 when I won the Open. I don't say the same thing all the time. If I'm playing super I'll say I can win. If I'm not, I won't. But I've never said anything intentionally disrespectful. I respect these guys. I just say what I believe is right, whether I'm talking to a friend or a reporter. I might say something to you very calmly, but when it appears in print it sounds harsh and opinionated.

"I'm not as popular as most guys, but I might be a better father. A lot of the guys who came on tour with me are getting divorces. I'm still happily married, and that's more important to me than sitting around the clubhouse shooting the breeze with other golfers after a round. I don't have that much in common with them. A lot of people think I'm aloof, but I don't mean to be. I don't socialize much because I would rather be with my wife and kids. My oldest boy has started school and my family can't travel with me as much, and that bothers me. When I decided years ago to be a great player who would last for a long time, I vowed not to let myself get too high or too low. You have to shepherd your energy. I don't even like to laugh at other people's jokes.

"It upsets some people that I don't play in many tournaments and don't practice as much as other players. They can't accept that I could take this approach and be successful. It's contrary to what they believe in, and they've had to hope I was a fluke."

Miller smiled, and a sense of humor surfaced. He giggled boyishly and said, "After the year I had in 1977, they ought to like me better."

Miller's principled world view leaves him wide open to snide remarks about "Johnny Miller, All-American boy." And there is nothing in his makeup to belie the image. He is the tour's Mr. Clean—he doesn't smoke, drink, curse or wink at strange girls. He plays pool—but only in his recreation room. He is an active Mormon who attends church twice on Sunday when he's home, for 90 minutes in the morning and 90 minutes in the evening, and frequently turns up at a week-night service in a tour city to give a short inspirational talk and field questions. "The best thing he does for the church," says a Mormon spokesman, "is set an example by his very lifestyle. He exemplifies the clean living that the church recommends." Tithing from his formidable earnings to the church surely doesn't hurt, of course.

"I expect a lot of myself because I've always been a leader," Miller has said. "In church, in Boy Scouts, with friends, whatever."

All of this came as a severe blow to the young single women of America who watched a 23-year-old Miller, wearing brightly hued clothes, his surfer's hair voguishly styled in a Prince Valiant cut, stalk dashingly across their television screens and into the national consciousness in the 1971 Masters, which he nearly won. They quickly learned Miller was a swinger on the golf course but not off it.

Of his colorful outfits, Miller says, "I like them because they cheer me up and they're good for color television. I enjoy experimenting with clothes." Especially, he might have added, clothes made by Sears, which pays him something like $170,000 a year to wear its latest shirts and slacks and pose for advertisements, Miller's slender, 6' 2" frame being almost mannequin-perfect for modeling. No company has used a golfer as extensively as Sears uses Miller, and one can envision even now the collector's-item Sears catalogs of the next century featuring the young Johnny Miller (will he ever age?) posing in leisure wear designed for breaking 65.

Making so much money off the course can be a two-edged sword, however. "It takes away from your golf time," Miller admits, "and it distracts you. It's my biggest problem. If I weren't making as much money as I am, a bad slump might drive me crazy, but as it is it's hard to get that worried about it. It's easy for me to sit back and figure I have nothing to worry about. I have plenty of money no matter what happens on the golf course. I'm set for life."

Actually, says Miller's business manager, Ed Barner, Miller does *not* have enough money to be set for life—not, at least, if he con-

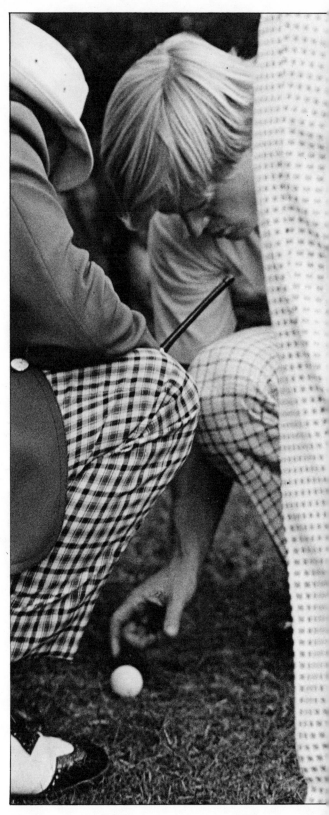

tinues living in the luxurious style to which he has become accustomed and not at modern inflation rates — but he *is* in wonderfully sound financial condition. "His big contracts, with Sears, Ford, Gillette and Princess Hotels, are solid and long term," says Barner. "A slump can cut into his exhibitions and personal appearances after a while."

In the final analysis, Miller's business involvements could rekindle his motivation to keep winning in golf, because the former ultimately, depend on the latter, and Miller—for all his homespun virtues—is uncommonly fond of expensive cars, boats and houses. "The way expenses are now, I can't afford not to be doing these other business things," he says on second thought.

It is his manager Barner, a Mormon like Miller and as close to him as anyone, who gives the clearest insight into the seeming enigma that is his client. "The thing is, he is a simple person, in the best sense of the word, and people try to make him out to be overly complicated. He doesn't need the adulation. He doesn't care if there's a courtesy car to meet him at the airport when he arrives for a tournament. His game goes up and down, and he doesn't know why and doesn't run to the practice tee. In a sport where everybody wants to be your friend, he's secure in his own company—he's most happy when he's alone. That's the real Johnny, and he isn't about to start pretending to be somebody he isn't. When he's through with the tour, I think he'll work actively in youth programs. He's really comfortable coaching youngsters who have some talent and want to become good golfers. He has the desire to teach, unlike most top players, and he has the patience."

If Johnny Miller can strike a meaningful balance between his professional life and his personal life, it is that temperament that could enable him to play with confounding brilliance for years and years to come. Some of the time, anyway.

Johnny Miller's off-tour life revolves around his family in Napa, Calif. Johnny and his wife Linda are shown here with three of their children: John, Kelly and Casi. At right, Johnny and little John try their hand at fishing in a stream on the Silverado Country Club near their home.

Miller may be domesticated, but he likes fast motor bikes and cars. At left, Johnny astride the dirt bike from which he fell in 1976, injuring his hand and missing the PGA Championship. Below, surfing in the glistening waters of Acapulco.

BOB TOSKI: Johnny Miller exemplifies the modern golf swing, in which the club is largely pulled during the downswing instead of being thrown or shoved at the ball. He produces a powerful pulling force essentially with his left knee, left arm and left hand. This left-side control is the outstanding feature of his swing, and it starts at address, when he applies more pressure with the last two or three fingers of his left hand.

Overall, he holds the club with only enough pressure to keep from dropping it, so his muscles will be long and relaxed during the swing

and he can generate good club-head speed. He says he grips the club as though it were a small bird.

Johnny advocates a palms-facing grip, which I would recommend to any player, but I would not recommend that you position the hands as far to your left as he does. The average player tends to slice the ball from left to right, and with this "weak" a grip, the slice would be aggravated. I'd rather see the hands turned 20 to 25 degrees to your right, more under the shaft. The V's formed between your thumbs and forefingers would point more or less toward your right

shoulder.

Actually, the word "weak" in golf is a poor term. A beginner or higher handicapper doesn't like it because it implies he isn't as strong as the next fellow. A good grip should be called "neutral," because it's in between "weak" and "strong." The left and right hands should be in a neutral position so they do an equal share of the work. When your grip is as weak as Miller's, you tend to take the club back in too upright a plane. And he sets up with his hands very low and close to his body and his knees very flexed, and that combination further en-

courages him to bring the club back too upright.

I like the way his arms hang freely at address. He swings to the top with admirable arm freedom. This is a good, big, full swing with an abundance of motion—but the motion is under control.

I would rather see him set up with more weight—60 to 70 percent—on his right foot, because at the top of his swing he is tilted to his left. His weight is hanging a little left, and from there most players would fail to shift the weight into the shot. They'd hit the ball dead right. Johnny hits it to the right when he stays

on his left foot too long on the downswing.

Although he is not ideal at the top, Miller usually makes the necessary compensations coming down. The left-side pulling action on his downswing makes up for his backswing deficiencies.

He initiates the downswing by sliding his left knee to his left, then pulls the club down smoothly with his left hand and arm. The left knee leads and the right knee follows. Driving his left knee laterally to start the downswing drops the club down out of the excessively upright plane it was in and puts it in posi-

tion to attack the ball from inside the target line—the best club path.

Unlike Miller, the average player throws the club back to the ball with his right side, uncocking his wrists too early and losing his leverage. Miller does not begin to uncock his wrists until his arms are more than halfway down.

Many golfers do not understand correct wrist action. They either overwork their wrists or else lock them ineffectually. Miller's wrist action is very nearly perfect. His left wrist hinges and unhinges freely at the base of his thumb, but the back of his left hand, left wrist

and left forearm remains straight throughout the swing, indicating firm left-hand control.

If you're observant, you notice that Johnny "sets the angle" — cocks his wrists — exceptionally early on the backswing. He almost sets his wrists and then swings. I think a good player can be firmer at the top if he sets the angle early, for he then can delay the uncocking of the wrists coming down. You may find it easier to cock your wrists more gradually, later in the backswing. The important thing is to get them cocked by the time you reach the top, then start down with your left knee and left arm and don't uncock the wrists until you approach the hitting zone. You can experiment in practice to determine how long you can keep your wrists cocked and still release them in time.

In conclusion, if we can learn one thing from Johnny Miller's swing, it is the unquestioned value of pulling the club down with the left side.

AL GEIBERGER

"Nice guys finish last"
   —Leo Durocher, 1946.
"Nice guys can win"
   —Al Geiberger, 1977.

If Al Geiberger is not the nicest guy on the PGA Tour, he has to be in the photo, as they say in horse racing. Nobody can remember the slender, laconic Californian ever throwing a club or blaming a missed putt on a camera click. That alone nearly makes the ever-smiling Geiberger one of a kind, but there's more; Geiberger actually goes out of his way to be nice to the fans and the press! In this modern era of overpaid and overpampered professional athletes, the preceding sentence deserves three exclamation points and Geiberger deserves three cheers.

Says Geiberger's good friend Dave Stockton, "If you're a golf buff and you want to meet a top player at work, walk up to Al on the course. He's unbelievable. If you want jokes and entertainment, follow Lee Trevino or Chi Chi Rodriguez. But if you want to learn about the game, follow Al. He's not on stage like Lee or Chi Chi, but he's sincere about wanting to help people. I've seen a fan clap at the wrong time—and Al goes over and gives him a putting lesson.

"His niceness comes out most doing exhibitions," continues Stockton, who is as ebullient as Geiberger is restrained. "Berger — that's what the pros call him—is the most patient man with other people I've ever seen. Most pros are very 'I-oriented' when they're doing an exhibition. They'll hit a lot of shots themselves. They hit them well and they awe the weekend golfers watching, but they don't teach them much. Al will go one-on-one with them and relate to *their* games and *their* problems. I love to do exhibitions with him because he's always willing to tackle the hard questions. Somebody will ask him where the hands should be at the top of the swing. Now answering

that question, without knowing how the 40 people standing there play, easily could help one of them and screw up the other 39. I'll pass it to Al, and he'll explain what he means in great detail, cautioning about the pitfalls, going over it and over it until he makes himself understood.

"Later we'll go out on the course and play a few holes with each foursome of amateurs. Al will go off on the first hole and I'll go off on the 10th, and invariably he'll make the turn two holes behind me because he's bending over backward to improve everybody's game. A couple of months later, one of those fellows can come up to Al in a restaurant on tour, drunk and overbearing, and Al will remember him and be pleasant and ask him all about his game. The only times Berger irritates me are when he gives too much of himself. He can be so considerate of other people that he doesn't think enough about himself."

To some extent, any successful athlete—any successful person—must be selfish, particularly in an individual sport. The better you get, the more selfish you have to be, because increasing demands are made on your time, many of them by importuning opportunists who want to hitch a ride on your rising star. Stockton and others close to him wondered for a long while whether Geiberger was tough and aggressive enough to fulfill his abundant potential. Those were the days when Leo Durocher was still winning, with a frown in his heart, and Geiberger seemed to lack a "killer instinct."

He since has demonstrated beyond a doubt that nice guys can finish first. He has won a major championship—the 1966 PGA—and a quasi-major—the 1975 Tournament Players Championship—plus nine other tournaments, and he has been tied for second in the U.S. Open twice. He is a member in lucrative standing of the game's Million Dollar Club. And in 1977, his 18th year on the tour, he did something that no one else had accomplished in the history of the tour, not Hogan or Snead or Palmer or Nicklaus, something that may never be equalled: he shot a 59.

The mind gropes for a forceful enough sporting analogy. A 3:30 mile run perhaps; hitting eight home runs in a doubleheader; scoring 150 points in a basketball game.

Wrote Jim Murray, the brilliant syndicated columnist, "There are certain things you don't believe in. The Easter Bunny. Campaign promises. The Abominable Snowman. A husband with lipstick on his collar. And a guy who tells you he shot a 59 on his own ball. Out of town, of course. Allen Geiberger, it says here, shot a 59 at Memphis. In front of witnesses. And his wife didn't keep score. And he played all 18 holes. Now that Geiberger has shot his 59, look for someone else to get the hang of it. Maybe even in your lifetime. If Geiberger does it again, his clubs shouldn't go to the Hall of Fame. They should go direct to the Smithsonian and hang next to Lindbergh's airplane."

The closer Geiberger's 59 is studied in retrospect, the greater its impact. Look at it this way. He averaged three and a third shots per

	4	15	16	17	18	OUT		TOTAL
	47	200	512	433	548	3615		7249
	4	3	5	4	5	36		72
	4	2	4	3	4			59
	-2	-3	-4	-5	-6	30	*Al Geiberger*	

NNY THOMAS MEMPHIS CLASSIC
OUND ~ FRIDAY, JUNE 10, 1977

hole at Colonial Country Club in Memphis, which *Golf Digest* ranks as one of America's 100 greatest courses. It's over 7,000 yards long and plays to a par of 72, and the next best score after Geiberger's historic 59 was a 65.

Geiberger hit every fairway and every green. He used only 23 putts and none was a tap-in; somebody with a sturdy pocket calculator computed that he sank 166 feet worth of birdie putts.

Johnny Miller, who knows what it is to get unconsciously hot, was boggled by Geiberger's putting. "If there was a set of greens I thought you couldn't do that on, it was those," he says. "They're Bermuda grass, which means you have to hit everything very firmly and truly. And Al had a late starting time, which means they were tracked up. You just don't make 12 putts of more than 10 feet in a round. It was phenomenal."

Geiberger attributed his spectacular putting to a lesson he took from Dave Stockton a fortnight earlier. Over dinner during the Atlanta tournament, Geiberger, who had missed the 36-hole cut for the second week in a row, said, "Dave, I can't make a putt. I cannot get the ball into the hole and I don't know why." The next day on the practice green, Stockton, himself a master putter, noticed that Geiberger was aiming to the right. When he adjusted his aim, Geiberger was primed for his 59, and as irony would have it he was paired that memorable day at Memphis with his tutor, Stockton.

Geiberger began his record round auspiciously enough, holing what he later called "a routine 40-foot birdie putt" on the 10th hole; the field was starting on both the first and 10th tees to expedite play. Through four holes he was two under par. Then came the turning point, the 14th hole, or Geiberger's fifth.

"I caught fire," he says, "which was a coincidence because I heard fire engines—there was a fire in the parking lot adjoining the 14th fairway. We had all kinds of excitement and several cars burned. Also on the 14th, a friend of mine who has a house alongside the fairway came out and gave me some crackers heaped with peanut butter an inch thick. Peanut butter's my favorite picker-upper."

(It will be remembered that the spindly 6'2", 175-pound Geiberger early on gave peanut butter social acceptability, snacking on it to keep up his energy on the course. He has a low blood sugar count and needs frequent fixes of protein. Asked why he chose peanut butter, he once replied, "Did you ever smell your golf bag after you car-

116

ried a tuna sandwich around in the hot sun?" He started packing peanut-butter sandwiches during the 1965 PGA Championship at Laurel Valley in Pennsylvania, Arnold Palmer's home course. "I was paired with Arnold and I knew we'd have such a huge gallery I wouldn't be able to get near a concession stand," he says. "My first wife was fixing a peanut butter and jelly sandwich for our daughter, and I asked her to wrap one up for me to take." Geiberger later got a contract with the Skippy Peanut Butter Company which he lost but then regained, by shooting his 59.)

Fortified by the peanut butter in Memphis, Geiberger birdied the last four holes on the back nine and then eagled the par-5 first hole, his 10th, when he sank a wedge shot from 30 yards out. He concedes that it was the one shot on which he conceivably was helped by the "preferred lies" rule in effect because of the harsh winter . . . players were allowed to lift and clean the ball on the fairway.

At this point, with five straight under-par holes in hand, Geiberger allowed himself to think about matching the PGA record for such things, which is eight. It had not occurred to him yet that he had a chance to break the 60 barrier.

He birdied the second and third holes to stretch the string to seven, but somehow missed a 13-foot birdie putt on the fourth hole, and said to himself, "Oh, well. There goes your chance to get your name in the record books." That shows how much Geiberger knew.

He parred the fifth hole and birdied the sixth, a 388-yard par-4, and

his gallery, by now 10,000 strong and sensing that it was going to have a great story to tell its grandchildren, began cheering wildly. Even Geiberger, who is usually about as excitable as the Statue of Liberty, broke out in goose bumps.

"While I was playing the sixth hole," he says, "I heard this spontaneous roar that sounded like it came from a football crowd. I birdied the hole from 13 feet, and that started the chant. One man in the gallery began to yell '59! 59! 59!' After a minute I realized what he meant. That's the first time I thought about breaking 60.

"I knew then I had to set 59 as my goal. You have to have something to shoot at. I have a tendency to back off when I get a good round going, and I have to push myself. It's like climbing a real steep hill with mud on your shoes. It gets harder and harder.

"I had three holes left and I had to birdie two of them. I birdied the seventh, a par-5, with a drive, a 3-wood, a pitch and a nine-foot putt. Now the entire crowd had picked up the chant: '59! 59! 59!'

"I had to make a birdie on one of the last two holes to set the record. I parred the eighth, two-putting from 20 feet, and that put it up to the last hole. The ninth at Colonial is a 403-yard dogleg left with a trap at the corner that can catch a shorter hitter like me, and I'm normally a left-to-right player. It must have been the adrenalin pumping or something, because I hit my drive right at the trap and carried it, which I had never done before. I was 125 yards from the pin. That's in between a 9-iron and a pitching

wedge for me. I decided to hit a soft 9-iron, and I put it eight feet from the hole.

"I looked at the putt, and the crowd went completely silent. The putt was uphill, left to right. Sometimes you look at a putt like that and you're not sure of the break. But that day I knew. I told myself I couldn't leave it short."

Geiberger addressed the putt in his upright, pigeon-toed stance, stroked it confidently—and ran it into the heart of the hole. Bedlam.

Typically, Geiberger was the least emotional person in the area, outwardly at least. Remembers Dave Stockton, "Jerry McGee and I were jumping up and down, and I looked over at Al and he came the closest I've seen him come to getting excited. He got his fist halfway clenched."

The average sports fan marveled at Geiberger's composure on that final putt, wondering how he could keep from "choking" or maybe fainting. Geiberger had a professional's explanation. "I'd been playing well all day, and that putt was just the culmination of that momentum," he said. "I knew it was the most important putt I'd ever hit, but I was in a good frame of mind. Your subconscious seems to take over. It's different being out there doing it than it is watching somebody else do it. When I'm home watching a tournament on television and somebody has a crucial putt, I think to myself that I'd choke to death in that spot. But when you're in that spot you think differently. If you've built your confidence all day by hitting good shots and holing a lot of putts, you don't worry about it."

Johnny Miller says you couldn't pick a better man for the Ultimate Pressure Putt than Geiberger. "I like to study people under pressure," Miller says. "They walk differently and talk differently. It's funny to see. But Al's a low-key guy who never looks like he's going to choke. I wasn't surprised he made that last putt."

Could Geiberger have shot 58 or even lower?

"Sure," he says. "There are a couple of 'could'ves' in every good round. I could've made the eight-foot birdie putt on the fifth hole I played, the 14th hole on the card. That's where we had all the commotion with the fire. On the hole before that, I left the 13-footer just short, right on line. All I had to do was hit it a tiny bit harder. But that's golf, right?"

It's also life-in-the-large, and the 59 changed Geiberger's very existence, forever. In the public's eye he went from being a nearly anonymous journeyman pro to a superstar. In truth he had played magnificently for the better part of two years before he shattered golf's equivalent of the sound barrier, but only his fellow players and a few insiders appreciated him; it takes a lightning bolt to change an image in mid-career, and for Geiberger it took a 59. Months later, he is still adjusting to the fame—and relishing it in his own restrained manner.

"Now people come up to me in airports where they never did before," he says. "I enjoy the attention, except when I'm four or five over par and somebody in the gallery asks me if I'm going to shoot 59 today. The fans call me Mr. 59, which has a nice ring to it. My lawyer and I are trying to copyright the name, and somebody had an idea to start a chain of restaurants that would be called Mr. 59. Those kinds of things keep rumbling up. I get a lot of invitations to fund-raising dinners on the West Coast to talk about the 59, and I'm glad to be able to help charitable causes.

"I'm still getting a lot of mail. I got one unbelievable letter from a lady back in Quincy, Massachusetts, who enclosed a clipping from her local paper—the horse racing results. On the day I shot 59, a horse in the eighth race—you're not going to believe this—a horse called Geiberger placed second. Paid $13.60 to place and $5.80 to show. First was Happy Lad. Third was Easy Par. Happy Lad Geiberger Easy Par. I never play the horses, but that's enough to make me a convert."

If anyone deserves belated fame and fortune, it is Al Geiberger. For eight years, after he won the 1966 PGA Championship, he floundered in almost total eclipse. To say he was in a slump is to understate the case. He missed the top 60 money-winning list for four years running. Before, he could play three weeks, take time off to regain his strength, then resume where he had left off. Not any longer. When he came back his timing would desert him. His putting suffered, then the rest of his game went on the wane. Fortunately, he teamed with Stockton for two wins in the old CBS Classic, the taped television series, or he would have been in financial quicksand.

And it wasn't just his golf. You name it and it went wrong for Geiberger. His game left him, his wife left him, his health left him. "The divorce probably would have happened anyway," he says, "but the bad golf may have accelerated it. Having my marriage break up wasn't a surprise, but it took a long time to figure it out. My first wife wasn't in love with the tour." The gnawing combination of golf and domestic tension set Geiberger's stomach to bleeding internally. He considered quitting the tour.

Then, from the depths of his own personal limbo, Al Geiberger fought back. He revived his game through his putting, firming up his stroke and setting up more behind the ball with his right shoulder low, in the Jack Nicklaus style. He took a course in positive thinking. He remarried, a bright, enthusiastic woman who wanted him to do for a living what he could do best—play tournament golf.

Late in 1974 Geiberger won the Sahara Invitational in Las Vegas, where he probably got more sleep than the rest of the field put together, and finally was rid of his prolonged slump even if it took him a while to realize it. It didn't register with him until he caught a cab to the airport late Sunday evening and the driver asked him who had won. Geiberger had to hesitate before he answered.

"I'd been asked that question many times by many cab drivers during those eight years," he says, "and the answer was always someone else besides me. Finally, I said, 'Hey, I won it.' That was my most satisfying victory, it came so much

harder than the others."

Through all his troubles, Geiberger remained uncomplaining and philosophical. He thought, like Francis Bacon, that "Prosperity is not without many fears and distastes; and adversity is not without many comforts and hopes." His comeback showed that he possessed a determination and resiliency that even many of his good friends had feared he lacked. In his own subdued fashion, Al Geiberger is a fighter.

"I'm not known as a great competitor, but inside I'm more competitive than people might imagine," he says. "I have a certain amount of bounce-back. It takes something to stimulate me, but when I'm in trouble, on or off the course, I usually have the resolve and patience to grind it out. I try to analyze a problem — golf or personal — realistically, without kidding myself. Problems usually aren't as complicated as we make them. Adversity can be good for you—can make you get off your fanny and get to work. A problem is an educational opportunity in disguise if you look at it constructively—there are a lot of potential lessons in any difficulty. I don't feel I ever reach bottom when I get down. I get down so far and then it's like an extra motor firing up and I fight back.

"Toward the end of that long slump I realized I either was going to have to play a lot and shape up my game, or get off the tour. The answer was easy. I had to get back to work. When you're younger and playing well, you get out of the habit of practicing hard, and as you

121

get older you have to renew your game. I see Gene Littler on the practice tee more now than I did 10 years ago—and he probably says the same thing about me. I come home and tend to get lazy—I tell myself I'm going to work on my wedge play, but a week later the bag's still covered—and my wife kicks me out of the house. She's encouraged me and helped me play better. When we got married she didn't know anything about golf, but she talked to a lot of the other players and their wives and they'd say, 'Geez, Al's one of the best players out here.' She'd accumulate all this and inject it into me."

Dave Stockton comments, "Al's more outgoing and a stronger person since he remarried."

Al agrees, saying, "I'm more aggressive now. I think it came through in shooting the 59. I used to be known as Mr. Consistency, rocking along in the middle of the field, never missing the cut but never winning. That pattern has changed. I'm missing cuts now but also shooting more low rounds."

There are those on the tour who believe Geiberger is the best player in the game today, Johnny Miller among them. "He has the most controlled swing out here," says Miller. "His swing is so pure, and he can putt, too. When I look at him I think he's the finest player we have."

Says Lou Graham: "Al has a fantastic, consistent attitude. When he walks off the 18th green you can't tell if he shot 65 or 75. He has a great, composed swing. He is the original play-within-yourself golfer."

Babe Hiskey says: "Al has a deceptive quiet confidence, and confidence breeds confidence. He has always known he's a better player than his peers, without saying so. That started when he was young and won the National Jaycee Tournament, and it's carried through on the tour."

Charlie Coody observes: "Tempo means everything out on the tour, and Al's tempo is exemplary."

Geiberger can talk about tempo until the sun sets in the East. He believes it is the most important factor in golf at any level, for the tour star or the once-a-week hacker. "Tempo," he says, "essentially is making a smooth, controlled swing in which everything builds up so that the maximum acceleration is reached in the hitting area. This sounds simple enough, but it obviously isn't, because most golfers swing faster than they need to and reach maximum acceleration at the wrong point in the swing. When I'm teaching a group of weekend golfers at a clinic, I find it helpful to tell them that they are issued only one fast moment per swing. It's impossible to have two fast moments in a swing, so make certain the one you get occurs in the hitting area. Swing smoothly."

Smooth-swinging Al Geiberger is 40 years old and his career, the third career he has led on the tour, should be on the downslide. It isn't. "His tempo and temperament will hold his game together when he's well past his prime," predicts Charlie Coody. "And it couldn't happen to a nicer guy."

Take that, Leo Durocher.

Back home in Santa Barbara, Calif., Al Geiberger goes about his off-course activities at the same leisurely pace he brings to golf. Above, Al and wife Lynn (holding their baby, Bryan) with children Lee Ann, John, Brent and Robby, putting. Above right, his office overlooks a backyard putting green. Below right, photography is Al's primary hobby. "I've got a lot of equipment," he says. "Just enough so I don't know what to use when it's time to take a picture."

BOB TOSKI: If you could set Al Geiberger's swing to music, you'd have a classic to rival Beethoven's best. It's a beautifully lyrical action, and I think it's the secret to his longevity and his ability to shoot low numbers. His tempo is smooth and consistent, and it doesn't speed up under pressure.

Some of this composure goes along naturally, I'm sure, with Al's relaxed lifestyle. He doesn't let himself get flustered and hurried, no matter what he's doing. He's that way on the golf course. He walks into the shot calmly, not as if he's going to try to hit it 5,000 miles. He

waggles calmly and starts his swing at a leisurely pace.

He has a perfect golf swing. He should attack the flagstick more often and he'd win more.

His posture at address is good. He tilts his upper body nicely, bending from the waist, and his arms hang freely. His weight looks pretty evenly distributed — it probably favors the right leg slightly, which I like. That will help him make a full, unrestricted backswing. Tall players particularly can learn from Al to bend from the waist and get their weight toward the balls of their feet. I have only one quibble

with his address position: I would rather see him not flex his knees quite so much. If his knees were flexed a little less, he could drive his legs better on the downswing.

On the backswing, he swings his arms up nice and freely, getting good extension of the left arm and club. The left arm stays firm without being stiff. His weight is over on his right side and he is working around the right knee. That's good. It's an arm swing to the top.

The club is just about parallel to the ground at the top, indicating good left-side control. Please observe the fullness of Geiberger's

backswing. He has the long, graceful, complete backswing that we see in every great player. A full swing lets him create clubhead speed on the downswing without overworking his hands and wrists. He has time to accelerate the club smoothly. In contrast, a player with a short, compact, quick swing is going to have to work very hard to get the swing velocity you need to play modern power golf. The tendency will be to use the hands and wrists too much and hit a lot of curve balls. Al has a splendid completeness of motion in his backswing, while maintaining control of the

club. This completeness of motion
is one reason he should play well
for a long time.

From the top of his swing, he
makes a well-paced, unhurried
transition from backswing to downswing. Al feels he starts his downswing with his left knee sliding toward the target, and we can see
what he means in these pictures.
Look at the separation that takes
place between the left knee and
the right knee early in the downswing.

Understand, though, that a player like Geiberger is not forcing his
lower-body movement in the down-

swing. Too many average players
today hear the top players talk
about using their legs, and they try
to emulate them without possessing
the timing or strength to succeed.
All they do is throw their swings
out of synch and lose control. You
have to be able to swing your arms
before you worry about your legs.

You can see the enviable con-
tainment of the angle between the
left forearm and the shaft of the
club on the downswing. He isn't
releasing the stored-up energy of
the swing too soon.

Al shows good extension of the
right arm through the ball because

he had such good retention of the clubshaft angle with the left arm earlier in the downswing. Left-arm retention creates right-arm extension.

He finishes in good balance because his weight got over to his left side quite well on the downswing.

The outstanding features of Geiberger's swing that the average player should study are: his posture, his well-paced arm flow both back and forward, his balance and his left-side leadership. But the most important thing you can learn from him has less to do with his mechanics than with his attitude. He is a brilliant example of a man who is smart enough to play within himself all the time. I'm sure he never goes at the ball 100 percent with his driver—I would say he swings with no more than 80 percent of his power. He has a keen sense of tempo, and he doesn't force any part of his swing. The smoothness and ease with which he swings the club are worthy of emulation by all of us. This man plays golf in a state of grace.

JACK NICKLAUS

Jack Nicklaus smokes as much as two packs of cigarettes a day—but he never lights up on the golf course.

A fellow smoker asked Nicklaus how he could abstain from smoking for half a day and longer.

Replied Nicklaus, "I don't think about it."

Nicklaus epitomizes mental discipline more dramatically than any other athlete in any sport. His willpower is so intense it is visible to the naked eye. We may expect him any day now to *stare* a putt into the hole from 20 feet.

(I was distracted from my work at this point in the story by a brush fire two doors away that drew the fire department. It struck me that Nicklaus, in my place, probably would not have heard the fire trucks and would have continued typing, his concentration intact).

Golf is, above all, the thinking man's game, and Nicklaus is the thinking man's golfer. It is the men-

tal dimension that sets him apart, that already has enabled him to set records for major championships won and for career money. He will tell you so, and so will his opponents, who consider him no less than the greatest golfer of all time.

Frank Beard, the full-time golfer and sometime journalist, recently picked a tour all-star team. He liked Al Geiberger with the driver, Ray Floyd with the fairway woods, Tom Weiskopf with the long irons. Beard worked his way through a half dozen other categories, and nowhere was Nicklaus mentioned.

"That must mean there is more to golf than striking the ball," Beard concluded. "There is—the mental side. Nicklaus is the best in this department. His ability to organize himself and maintain his discipline, concentration and composure is unparalleled. I've never seen Jack select the wrong club, hit a stupid shot or lose his cool. If you put together a composite best golfer—

the best driver, best putter and so on—Nicklaus could give him two a side."

The implication should not be that Nicklaus leaves a great deal to be desired physically. His physique, coordination and game all are near-bionic.

He is blessed with massive legs, the generators of his awesome power. "His thighs are 29 inches around," says Dave Hill, "which just happens to be the size of my waist."

Nicklaus is perhaps 15 yards shorter off the tee than he was five years ago, but still can move the ball as far as he has to. His is an entirely resourceful power.

Nicklaus isn't the longest driver on the tour but he's probably the smartest—and that's more telling. He is the game's preeminent player largely because of his resourceful tee shots. He plans his play on a hole to make it as easy as possible, always knowing exactly what he wants to do.

Says one of his peers, "I've never seen Jack hit a stupid tee shot. His ability to attack a hole is unmatched."

Nicklaus explains: "Playing for position is the key to effective driving on nine out of 10 holes. I try to hit the ball to a specific section of the fairway, not just onto the fairway in general. I always think positively, selecting a target to hit rather than an area to avoid.

"Remember that your prime purpose on the tee shot is to place the ball in the best possible position for your second shot. I pick a flat target area, so I won't be playing my second from a sloping lie. If I don't have to hit a driver off the tee to reach the green in regulation figures, I often hit a 3-wood or even a long iron, instead, for control."

Nicklaus can hit his irons higher than anyone else on this particular planet, which means he can land a long iron softly — "as softly as a butterfly with sore feet" — it has been said on the tour.

Further, Nicklaus is the strongest player in golf out of the rough. He can bludgeon the ball onto the green from 180 yards away with his forceful, upright swing when others can only chop the ball out short.

Nicklaus' hand-eye coordination is fully as impressive as his power. Try this little test on a friend. Have him put his hands out in front of him, palms facing, six inches apart. Hold a dollar bill just above the gap between his hands, let the dollar go and see if he can catch it. Nicklaus can snare the dollar nine times out of 10, a facility that could keep him in pocket money if he needed it.

As a youngster, Nicklaus was a good all-round athlete, playing quarterback in football and doing the kicking, then playing basketball in the winter and baseball in the spring. He committed himself to golf because it was easier to play by himself in the summer; he didn't have to round up a gang of kids to have a game.

"Golf was the only sport at which I could try to become a complete player by myself," he told Ken Bowden, his Boswell, in a searching *Golf Digest* interview. "When I got the golf bug I went overboard. It was nothing for me to go out in the morning in the summertime, hit golf

balls for an hour or two, go play 18 holes, come in, have lunch, hit more golf balls, go out and play 18 more holes, come back in and hit more balls until dark. That was a very normal routine for me during my early teens.

"In the summertime, I doubt if I would miss three days of doing that. We never took vacations. I never went to camp as a kid. I played golf. That's what I wanted to do."

The point is that Nicklaus is a good athlete. Even today, when golf easily could become his entire life, he enjoys playing tennis during the off-season on the neatly manicured grass court in his yard near Palm Beach, and he has been known to prepare for a golf tournament by competing the previous Saturday in a nine-hour decathlon session with his sons, plus other neighborhood youngsters and Mickey Neal, athletic director at Benjamin Junior High School in North Palm Beach.

Actually limited to nine events ("I made them quit at 9:30 when dinner was ready," smiled wife Barbara), the competition included golf, tennis, Ping-Pong, one-on-one basketball, free throw shooting, pool, punt-pass-kick, swimming and a 40-yard dash.

"You should have seen those two fathers trying as hard as they could to beat the kids," Barbara chuckled. "They *think* they're still all-round athletes anyway."

In golf, the Nicklaus coordination shows in a disciplined putting stroke that makes him the best fast-greens putter in the world and also the best pressure putter. Who else could take the putter away from the ball as deliberately as Nicklaus? If you had to choose a man to try one putt for everything you own — house, car, swizzlestick collection— you would have to pick Nicklaus.

He is virtually impervious to pressure, which brings us back to the mental capacity that makes Nicklaus No. 1. "People don't appreciate that he thinks his way around a golf course better than anybody else," says Hale Irwin. A dozen players hit the ball at least as purely as Nicklaus. There may be better putters day in and day out. But no one approaches him in mental discipline, and ultimately it's a mental game.

"I define concentration," says Nicklaus, "as the ability to make my body do what my mind wants it to do. When I'm able to think clearly what I want to do and then make my body do it, that's when I'm concentrating."

Nicklaus suffers lapses in concentration, of course—if only about as often as you and I inherit a million dollars or jump over the moon —but almost never is he careless. As a youngster he developed the ability to focus on every shot as if it were his last.

From the time he took up golf at 10, Nicklaus has hit every single practice shot as if it counted. Consider what that means over the course of 26 years and literally hundreds of thousands of practice balls. *Every shot is important.*

In practice rounds before a tournament, most pros will casually drop and hit a second ball if a first shot doesn't come off. Not Nicklaus. He knows you get only one try

when the tournament starts, and everything he does is geared to winning the tournament. Taking every shot seriously is a way of life with him.

As a result, Nicklaus is much less susceptible to final-round pressure than his rivals. Because he has treated every shot with total respect for so long, his anxiety level doesn't go up in the home stretch of a tournament. His mind is clear to deal with one shot at a time.

Nicklaus rarely shoots 74 or 76 and beats himself in the last round.

To beat him, the other fellow has to play better than he does—which is asking a lot. Tom Watson held off Nicklaus in the 1977 Masters and British Open by playing the best golf of his life; Jack played well enough to win most major tournaments.

Nicklaus' record in the majors is little short of incredible. Through 1977, he had played in 63 major championships and won 16. He was second or tied for second 13 times and was third or tied for third another eight times! There has never

Dogging the footsteps of Nicklaus, caddie Angelo Argea mirrors the intensity of his boss.

been a record like it. Behind it is Nicklaus' supreme power of intellect.

Dr. David Morley, a psychiatrist who knows Nicklaus (non-professionally), marvels at the clock-like workings of his mind:

"He has this tremendous ability to concentrate under conditions where most of our minds would be going a hundred ways at once. It has to be his greatest single asset. A primary factor is the continual application of intellect, rather than emotion, to the job confronting him. He controls every move to a very specific end. There are no false starts, no blank spots, no slipping into neutral gear. The clutch of his mind responds quickly without pause or hitch."

If Nicklaus hits the odd bad shot, he summarily analyzes what went wrong, files the information away, and puts the shot out of his mind. He doesn't let the bad shot discourage him or affect his handling of the next shot.

Says a graying veteran of the pro tour, "Imagine that the mind is a quart jar. Nicklaus makes sure the jar is always full of positive thoughts — intentions of hitting good shots. The rest of us tend to fill the jar at least half way with negative thoughts. We're thinking what can go wrong with a shot rather than what should go right. His mind is so permeated with the task at hand, there's no room for negatives."

Tom Weiskopf tells the story of being teamed with Nicklaus during the 1975 Ryder Cup Matches and joking as Nicklaus lined up a 15-foot putt, "You've never missed one of those in your life, have you Jack?"

Nicklaus' icy blue eyes drilled his friend and Nicklaus said, "Not in my mind, I haven't."

Many of his rivals cannot believe how little Nicklaus practices. He will warm up for 20 or 30 minutes before a round. After a round, when he believes practice is most productive, he will return to the range if he wants to work on something in particular. I have seen him hit five balls, find what he wanted and go home.

"I don't beat balls for the sake of beating balls like so many guys out there," he says.

The truth is he doesn't have to. The years of thoughtful practicing, respecting every shot, have matured his swing and concentration to the point they need only minor tune-ups, not major overhauls.

An imposing by-product of Nicklaus' physical and mental ability is his almost unassailable self-confidence. "He believes he has an absolute and inalienable right to win," says a PGA tour executive. "He has never really experienced failure, and he has no fear of losing —or winning." That consummate confidence, stopping just short of arrogance, has characterized all the great golfers, from Vardon to Jones to Hogan to Palmer to Nicklaus. They felt—had to feel—they could figure a way to win under any circumstances.

"Nicklaus is the only man out there who can have two or three bad holes, then promptly turn his day around with two or three birdies," says another leading money winner.

Never was Nicklaus' capacity for righting a sinking ship more emphatically evident than in the last round of the 1976 World Series of Golf. Going to the third tee Sunday, Nicklaus was three strokes ahead of the field and looking as if he could beat the field's best ball the rest of the way.

But Nicklaus bogeyed the third hole and then played the fourth like a man wearing a strait jacket. He took four to get down from behind the fourth green, made a double-bogey 6 and tumbled back into a tie for the lead with Japan's Takashi Murakami.

Most golfers, their game plans slipping away from them under fourth-round pressure, become cautious or angry. In either case, they are in no state of mind to start a comeback. They have lost their mental discipline.

Nicklaus didn't miss a beat. He parred the fifth hole, hit a towering 4-iron approach shot three feet from the cup to birdie the sixth, nearly birdied the 215-yard seventh and birdied the long eighth with a second shot that deserves its own paragraph.

Nicklaus' drive on the eighth disappeared deep into the left rough. He faced a 190-yard shot into the wind from a downhill lie in thick grass. Taking a 7-iron (that is not a typographical error), he played an incredible low, British-type shot that ran onto the green and almost went in the hole. Birdie three. End of tournament.

There are assorted other instances of Nicklaus rescuing a round that looked to have gone down in flames. In the first Jackie Gleason Inverrary tournament, he was paired with "Cigar Joe" Campbell and began his opening round double bogey, bogey, double bogey.

Nicklaus said to Campbell, "Isn't this is a *bleep* of a way to start a tournament? I'll probably end up blowing it by a shot." Which is exactly what he did.

"How's that for confidence?" asks Steve Reid, a PGA official who was playing the tour at the time. "It never crossed his mind that he was out of it. I'd have been looking for a phone booth."

Nicklaus defines confidence as "feeling sure of your ability to do something" and adds, "If I have it in my head that I'm going to do something, knowing I have the ability to do it is confidence."

When you're talking about Nicklaus' mental sets, you cannot leave out his competitiveness. His friends talk about him as the most competitive animal they know, whether he's playing the tour or playing a neighborhood pickup softball game.

Nicklaus exudes the killer instinct peculiar to sports immortals. The breakfast of champions is not cereal; it's your opposition.

One of my favorite writers, William Price Fox, points out that Nicklaus needs a new nickname. Fox says "The Golden Bear" doesn't work because bears are not essentially killers. In Mexico, he says, Nicklaus would be known as "El Tigre"—the tiger—which would be fitting because tigers are ruthless stalkers that annihilate their prey.

"In one of Sugar Ray Robinson's fights," writes Fox, "his second-round victim let out the sad lament, 'I never knew the ring could be that small.' Against a killer the ring is always that small. That's the way it should be. You feel your strength draining as the suspicion hardens into the ice cold fact that you're not going to be admired for being there, but simply and humiliatingly man-handled and disposed of. This is what Dempsey and Louis and Jones and Hogan did in style for years. And it is what Nicklaus is doing today."

Happily for golf, Nicklaus' killer instinct comes garbed in exemplary deportment. The game is fortunate to have him as its hero. He does not complain openly, he does not show temper conspicuously, he does not try to take advantage of the rules—which he knows practically down to the last footnote.

Perhaps the most remarkable feature of Nicklaus' entire career is the quiet grace with which he endured, as a mere teenager at first, overweight and underexposed, the obscene taunting of fans who resented his displacing Arnold Palmer as king of the golfing hill. Not once did Nicklaus respond in kind, not around newsmen, at any rate.

In later years, his graciousness was once put to a test during the Westchester Classic. The weather was a steam bath—temperature 102 degrees, humidity close behind. By now trim and popular with a resolute diet, Nicklaus was sought out on the clubhouse porch by an exuberant fan carrying two beers, one in each hand. The fan embraced Nicklaus—and spilled both beers on him.

Inquired Nicklaus with cool evenness, "Why don't you have another beer?"

As far as I can see, Nicklaus is the best loser in sports. I have never heard him offer an excuse for not winning. His remarks after his frustrating defeat by Watson in the 1977 Masters were typical. "No matter what I did out there, somebody was always doing something a little bit better," he said. "Tom played great golf and deserved to win."

His sense of humor came through in one piece. When a writer wondered if losing was a disaster, Nicklaus grinned ruefully and said, "It is, when it's a lovely spring afternoon and you don't have anything else planned."

Nicklaus feels defeat keenly, though. He says, "I do not like to lose. It's as simple as that. Pride is probably my greatest motivation, because I just refuse to get beat, I can't stand to get beat, and I hate to have somebody come along and beat me. But I don't mind losing if a guy plays better than I do. I get beat a lot. That's one nice thing about golf—it's a humbling game. Golf is the only sport where, if you win 20 percent of the time, you're the best. In other sports you must win as much as 90 percent of the time to be the absolute best.

"The only thing that embarrasses me is not giving 100 percent. If I ever stopped giving 100 percent, it would run me out of the game. If I give it all I have, and I lose to somebody who plays better, then I don't mind losing so much. But it still hurts."

Nicklaus' sporting attitude gives golf the best reputation of any major professional game. In an age when lawyers seem to be taking over the world and too many athletes jump higher for a quick dollar than they do for a line drive in baseball or a rebound in basketball, Nicklaus combines the best of the past and present.

Tennis in recent years has been beleaguered by under-the-table payments to star players and winner-take-all television matches that in truth weren't. Nicklaus consistently has eschewed promotions that tend to cheapen the game and its major championships. When he had a chance to play Johnny Miller for a million dollars a few years ago, he quickly and decisively turned it down, and explained why. He didn't feel it was in the best interests of golf.

Not that Jack needs money for his next swimming pool. He is a mil-lionaire, and it often is speculated that he is hurting his golf career by running a varied business empire. He spends considerable time designing golf courses, for example, such as his Muirfield Village masterpiece in Ohio.

My own opinion—free of charge —is that Nicklaus' other interests benefit his golf and finally will prolong his career. No player can compete much more than half the time and stay at the top on today's year-round, world-wide golf schedule. And Nicklaus has always paced himself intelligently, both to be in peak form for important tournaments and also to have time for his family (he makes it a policy not to be away from home for longer than two weeks) and other interests. His is the sort of active mind that must have diversity or else he quickly becomes bored. His mentality is such that he can focus 100 percent on one activity—and only one at a time—but can shift that searing focus to a wholly different subject as readily as you can switch on a light.

Let me give you an example. I wrote a film script about Nicklaus' first Memorial Tournament. He wanted several additional points made about the golf course. The first chance I had to discuss the film with him was at the World Series of Golf. Nicklaus noticed me during the Saturday round, as he was moving in the lead, and said he'd see me afterward in the press tent.

He came into the tent, reviewed his round in shot-by-shot detail for the assembled writers, and on his way from the tent to the locker room went over the film with me.

He had seen the 30-minute film only once, but he remembered every key picture and line, and he made his suggestions—point by lucid point — in five minutes, almost on the run. Then he left and went to a business meeting on another, unrelated matter. Don't tell me it hurt his golf. He ran away with the tournament.

"Bob Jones had that same kind of mind," said the late golf impressario Fred Corcoran. "He could practice law in the morning and win the U.S. Open in the afternoon."

Says Jack, "A normal week when I'm home would probably be two full days and three half days in the office, with golf a couple of afternoons and a little fishing maybe one morning. Usually, I'm in the office some part of every day.

"I really enjoy it. There is a lot of mental stimulation in golf, but it's channeled. I need more mental stimulation than just one channel. I love the atmosphere of business . . . the discussions, the decision-making, the problem-solving, the need to use your brain. I find business invigorating. And the things I've learned! Really, it's been like a complete college graduate course.

"If I know which end of the club to hold when I come back on the tour after a layoff, I can handle the non-golf activities easily. In fact, it's mentally beneficial for me to get away and do something else, so long as I know I can go right back and pick up my game again. But if golf is a new game when you start back, then you have problems."

Deane Beman, the PGA tour commissioner, says, "The first few years he was on the tour, Jack let Mark McCormack handle his business interests, and Jack had no distractions. When Jack took over his own business affairs he was so well organized he was able to pursue other fields with the same intensity he brings to golf. But remember that his mental discipline started with his golf game."

At the summit, golf has always been a game of the mind, a contest not so much against outside forces as against oneself. It is his superiority in the mental aspects that makes Jack Nicklaus clearly preeminent. As one of his fellow pros puts it, he plays best that six-inch course between the ears.

141

Jack Nicklaus has never let golf become an all-consuming passion. He finds time for other diversions, many involving his family. At left, he enjoys snorkeling and tennis. Above, young Nan Nicklaus exhibits her skill on the trampoline for the family. Watching intently are Jackie, Gary, Jack, wife Barbara, Michael and Steve.

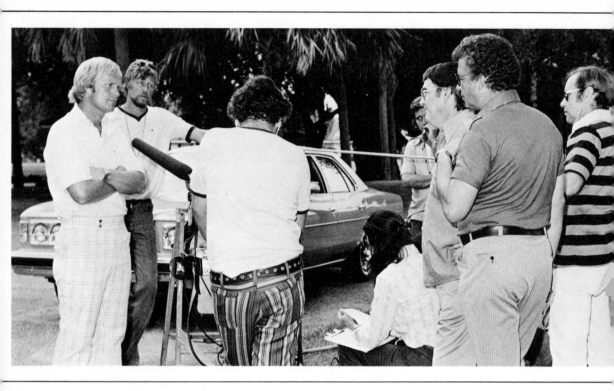

North Palm Beach, Fla., where Jack Nicklaus lives, is the nerve center of his business empire—the home of the prospering Golden Bear Enterprises. Above, Jack makes a Pontiac commercial. At right, the well-dressed business executive in his office.

Nicklaus' penchant for designing golf courses has led him to far-away projects. Below, he puts the final touches on his reworking of the Australian Golf Club in Sydney, home of the Australian Open. Looking down is Kerry Packer, an Australian communications executive who is a major sponsor of the tournament. Seated at left are Chuck Perry, president of Golden Bear Enterprises, and John Montgomery, an American who is tournament director of the Australian Open.

BOB TOSKI: Jack probably does more good things in his swing than any player in the history of the game. His fundamentals are as sound as any I've seen.

Look at Jack's posture — he's hanging out over the ball so he can swing the club more up and around his body instead of just around his body. He swivels his head to the right to start the backswing smoothly.

Jack takes the club straight away from the ball, like most good players. He swings his hands and arms and allows his shoulders to respond to the force of his club—he

lets his body pivot instead of *forcing* his body to pivot. Observe the early part of his swing going back. The club passes his right foot with little apparent hip or shoulder turn.

When he finally starts moving the club inside the target line, then his hips and shoulders respond to that motion and coil around and up.

We hear a lot about his left heel coming up on the backswing. Why is his left heel off the ground? Because he was taught to allow his left heel to come off the ground. He was taught by Jack Grout to let the force of his arms swing around

and up. He gets nicely behind the ball at the top of his swing. He was taught to "reach for the sky"—and the momentum of the arms swinging up pulls the heel off the ground. It's very difficult to swing your arms skyward and keep your heel downward, and the average player should not try to keep the heel down.

Jack puts his heel back down at the start of his downswing. His footwork is magnificent. The key to his footwork on the downswing is how slowly and smoothly he takes the club to the top of the swing. He gives himself time to move his feet.

You can't run as fast as you can throw, can you? It's evident that your legs can't move as fast as your arms, so the more time you give your legs to move forward — the slower you swing your arms back —the better chance you have. It's like a pitcher throwing a baseball, or a quarterback throwing a football. He gets back on his right leg, steps forward onto his left leg, and gets into position to throw. He needs time to do that. He doesn't want to rush into throwing.

In fact, in a player of Jack's caliber I see the legs working forward *even before the arms are finished*

going back. That little bit of a "downcocking" is the secret of the great golf swing. That is an infinitely exacting execution that few people in this world ever attain.

The upper body is still winding around and back, and the legs are moving forward a fraction of an instant earlier. The upper body then reacts to the legs moving, with the left arm leading and the right arm passive, and gets in position so these players can maintain what we call a retention of the angle between the shaft and the left forearm—can contain the wrists and hands until they're in the hitting zone, where they can uncock at just the right time for maximum power.

Jack's very consciously a legs player, but this is a point of departure for the average player. The average player should be taught first to swing his arms and hands to control the force of his swing. I've always said that you have to feel the force and not force the feel.

Would I change anything in this wonderful Jack Nicklaus golf swing? If I were to ask him to do one thing, I would ask him to work around his right leg more—let his arms simply swing around his body and not try to reach up for the sky

quite as much. I like his posture, but he is hung over the ball so much he almost overdoes it. He could get so close to the ball that the only thing he could do is take the club vertically straight up. That would be the only change I would make, and that change probably will come naturally. I can see his backswing changing as a result of time. But he wants an upright swing to hit the ball high, and his action is nearly ideal.

Jack's upright plane is going to make him a better player for a longer time than a player with a flat swing, because if you have a higher arc you have more time to build momentum. When the arc gets flatter as you get older, you put more stress on your arms, and if your arms don't have time to build leverage and momentum, then you start trying to create motion with your wrists and hands, and those are the weakest links in your body.

Studying these pictures, I can understand why Jack's record is the greatest yet.

GARY PLAYER

Phil Ritson, one of his early teachers, remembers sharing a room with a 16-year-old Gary Player and waking in the morning to find Player staring into a mirror and declaring, "I'm going to be the greatest golfer in the world! I'm going to be the greatest golfer in the world!" He must have said it 50 times, Ritson remembers, and then he went out and practiced sand shots by the dawn's early light.

Player, one of a very few golfers who could be ranked great, had lost none of his zealous determination at age 41. It is easy to imagine him today repeating his vows in front of a mirror or out slapping sand shots as the rest of us slumber heedlessly through the pre-breakfast hours.

Depending on the day you ask him, he speaks with iron resolve and eyes that burn with the intensity of automobile headlights of one towering goal or another: He wants to win more tournaments than anybody else ever, he wants to complete a second cycle in the four major championships, he wants to strike the ball as purely as Ben Hogan. And he continues to compete tirelessly around the world week after week in his unwavering quest for immortality.

The most successful foreign golfer ever to play in America, South Africa's Player has made his reputation and his fortune here for the most part, but he has also proved himself under all kinds of conditions elsewhere. He has won on five different continents—in the same year! No one has ever done as well outside his homeland as Player. He has prevailed in Japan, Spain, Australia, Egypt, Brazil and several times in Britain, among other places. Most good golfers' games, like a lot of good wines, do not travel well. Player can compete on any course anywhere, from storied, understated Muirfield on the Scottish seaside to young, spectacular Muirfield Village on the Ohio countryside.

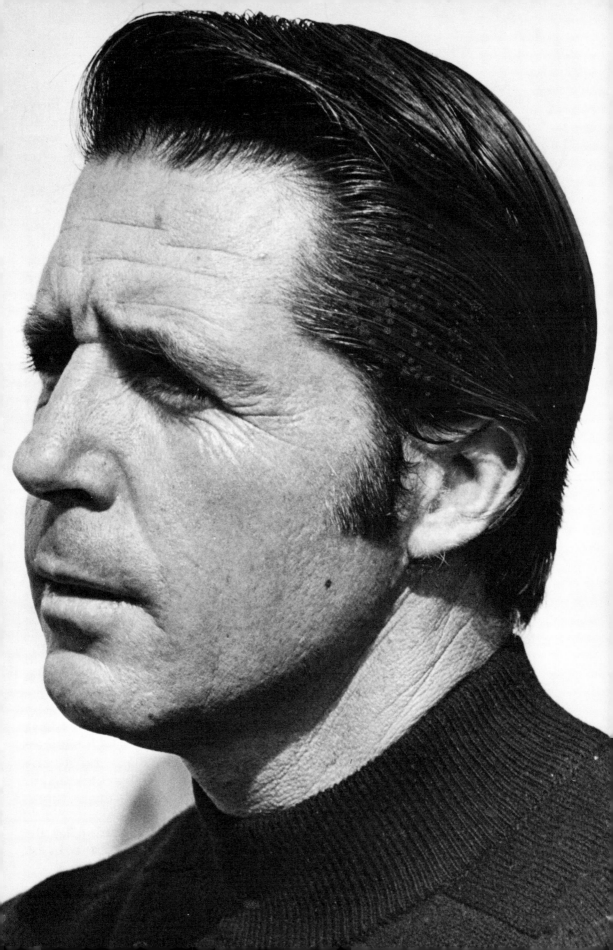

"Of all of us," observes David Graham, the bright young touring pro from Australia, "he most deserves his success. Sometimes he carries his positive thinking too far —he's the only guy I know who can shoot 80 and say he hit the ball super—but then he's a great self-promoter. He's a credit to the sport, and his record is better than people realize. He's won the four major tournaments, and he's won major tournaments 15 years apart."

I buy Graham's assessment. We have had enough lightweight debate over Player's sincerity in matters of physical fitness, race relations and international diplomacy. There is no denying that his enthusiasm can overflow the banks of thoughtfulness and spill out into ridiculous overstatement. For instance, he says with revival-tent fervor, "I know I've worked harder than any human being my age, not just at golf but at developing my body, my public relations, my mind." A *truly* well-developed mind might not make a claim like that.

A course on which Gary has just shot 67 always seems to be the toughest he has ever overcome. An almost compulsive competitor, he has to have a test of character. If he sees no obstacle to clear, he will erect one to keep up his interest. At positive thinking he could give Norman Vincent Peale two a side.

"You have to understand Gary," says Jack Nicklaus, his long-time friendly rival. "He simply exudes enthusiasm. He's forever telling you he's playing his best golf ever. That's a nice attitude, but you have to take it for what it is. It's his way of charging himself up."

We should appreciate that Player is essentially a golfer and should be judged by us, as golf followers, essentially on his record. It is on the course, single-mindedly confronting—almost embracing—his next problem, that the real Gary Player reveals himself. His career is studded with 24-karat accomplishments.

Player in 1974 just might have come closer to winning the Grand Slam than anyone yet has. In 1953 Ben Hogan won three of the four major tournaments but didn't enter the fourth, the PGA Championship. Seven others have won two majors in a season since the Masters began in 1934: Craig Wood, Sam Snead, Jack Burke, Arnold Palmer, Jack Nicklaus, Lee Trevino and Tom Watson. Did any of them come as close to the slam as Player? He won the Masters from behind and the British Open from in front (his seventh and eighth majors overall), was tied for the lead in the U.S. Open after two rounds and was never more than five shots from the top in the PGA, matching the tournament record of 64 in the second round.

Player also won at Memphis in this country in 1974 and took six titles abroad to go over 100 for his pro career. He capped the year by winning the Brazilian Open where he shot a shocking 59. "It was my best year," he says, "and maybe the best year anyone ever had." All this the year after major surgery,

Player is widely regarded by his peers as the best sand player in the game.

152

more serious than most of us realized, took him out of action and out of our field of attention.

As usual, Player came back from adversity with redoubled desire, in one case flying for two solid days and nights and disembarking from the plane to go straight to the course and win another tournament. He says he has traveled a total of four million miles to play golf, and that is one record that should outlive us all. Unlike most other superstars, he still practices as much as he plays, devising competitive games to make himself concentrate. He might hit chip shots, for example, until he sinks three dozen, come hell, high water or darkness.

Where does he get his dedication? How does he sustain it?

To reply, Player flashes back to his boyhood. We are eating in a New York restaurant, Player with the meticulousness he applies to everything, cutting his steak into uniformly small bites and drinking warm water laced with lemon juice to aid his digestive processes. He talks of the death of his mother when he was 8 and the insistence then and thereafter of his father, a good golfer who was a mine captain in the gold mines of Johannesburg, that an affirmative attitude is the only response to a challenge. That was his first exposure to positive thinking.

At Muirfield in 1959 (left), Player, age 23, won the British Open for the first time. Nine years later at Carnoustie (right), he did it again. Still a third British Open title came in 1974, at age 38.

An older brother, Ian, further influenced him at an early age to try harder than the rest, Player says in his book, "Gary Player: World Golfer." Ian, who refused to be held back by a chronically bad knee, laid out a five-mile track where the two ran together. One day the young Gary wearied and sank to his knees, wheezing that he couldn't finish.

He wrote, "My lungs felt as if they would burst. Without any warning Ian yanked me to my feet and cuffed me on the side of the head. 'What do you mean you can't make it, man?' he exploded, his face flushed red with anger. 'You can do anything you want to. Remember that. There's no room for *can't* in this life.' I'll never know how I did it, but even though my feet felt like they were weighted down with lead and my leg muscles were knotted with pain, I ran the rest of that five miles without stopping for anything. Believe me, I was cured of ever threatening to quit in front of Ian again."

It was Ian, Gary says, who gave him his first golf club, which Ian had whittled from a stick. Amazingly, Gary did not take up the game until he was 15, having busied himself with soccer, cricket, rugby, swimming and track and field. An outstanding all-round athlete, he parred the first three holes he played and was hooked for life.

The teaching professional at the course where he and his father played was Jock Verwey, who has a son, Bob, and a daughter, Vivienne, about Gary's age. The three youngsters frequently played rounds together and got free in-struction from Jock. Bob later became a touring pro, and Gary, who quickly got down to scratch, later married Vivienne.

In his early days as a tournament player, Gary recalls, nobody thought he could win. The little South African (he is only 5'8" and 150 pounds today) had gone to England to play, and the vaunted experts there agreed that his swing was too flat and his grip too strong.

But Norman Von Nida, the crusty little Australian who is famous for his minority opinions and his teaching record, came up to Player and told him he was going to be a great champion. Shocked, Player asked why.

"Because," replied Von Nida, "you've got *IT*." Meaning, apparently, a look of irrefutable determination.

Von Nida then arranged for Player to travel to Australia, where Player stayed and studied with Von Nida and won a big tournament, a victory that gave him the financial base to get married. When Player traces the important influences on his life, he eagerly gives credit to Von Nida, from whom he learned his sophisticated sand technique, among other things. Player is possibly the most accomplished sand player in the world—he has been known to *aim* at bunkers.

Fifteen years ago Von Nida told Player he could make more money breeding horses than being the best golfer in the world. Today, Gary is heavily into horse breeding and says, "There is a lot of sense in what he said."

Player early on made Ben Hogan another hero. He still reveres him, although there has been friction between the two. Hogan's example convinced Player that a small man without great natural ability could build a winning golf game through tenacious practicing and self-application.

"I promise you Hogan knows more about striking a golf ball than any man who ever lived," Player says. "If I could just ask him five questions and get his answers I'd be a lot better player than I am."

You no doubt have heard the story about Player calling Hogan overseas at his equipment plant for help with his swing. The conversation is supposed to have gone something like this:

"Mr. Hogan, this is Gary Player. I would like to ask you a question about the swing."

"Gary, who do you work for?"

"The Dunlop Company."

"Well, call Mr. Dunlop." Click.

About the call, Player says, "I wasn't put out that he refused to give me advice. If you ask for something for nothing, you have to expect a tough answer. My feelings were hurt when he hung up on me. But when the two of us were inducted into the Hall of Fame in Pinehurst later, he was most charming to me and my wife."

Player believes Hogan, who has a photographic memory, was rankled over a business misunderstanding that took place when Player first came to this country in 1955. Player then had only $3,000 to his name, he says. The Hogan Company offered him $2,800 to play its equipment. At the same time, First Flight offered him $9,000. Player meanwhile was being coun-

seled by a man in England (Mark McCormack now manages him) and says he called the Englishman and asked what he should do.

"He told me, 'By all means, you must take the $9,000.' Then I asked him if he would arrange things for me with First Flight and explain to the Hogan company what I was going to do. He said he would, but I later found out he never told the Hogan company anything. I was just 19 and had no business experience or I would have made sure it was handled properly. I think that caused the tension between me and Hogan."

Many experts suspect Player has always fought a pull-hook shot pattern because he wants to swing shorter and flatter like Hogan. Player periodically proclaims victory over his roundhouse hook, but still hooks dramatically at times.

The tense-looking Player's game invariably is less imposing on the face of it than that of any other top player, what with his hooking and finishing his swing off balance and using unorthodox strategy. He can shoot 68 and appear to be shooting 86. But he frequently brings off daredevil recovery shots, and it doesn't hurt him to be off balance at the finish of his swing as long as he's in balance when he contacts the ball, and his strategy has a way of working out.

Hale Irwin, another champion, shakes his head aptly summing up Player's game. "You can learn things from all these great players," he says, "but Gary could drive you crazy if you were paired with him often enough. I played with him the first two rounds of the British Open once and he hit a lot of 3-woods and long irons off the tee that I couldn't understand. He left himself second shots that were harder than his first shots. But the name of the game is scoring, and he knows it. He has a great pair of hands, and I have to think he was born in the sand the way he comes out of it."

Says Phil Ritson, his early mentor, "Gary has the willpower to completely blot a bad shot out of his mind. He forgets it immediately and begins planning the next one. Every shot is a separate little game with him."

Perhaps most crucially, Player gives every shot his utmost respect and concentration whether it's a long trouble shot or a tap-in putt. "The thing I admire so much about him," says Byron Nelson, "is that he just never wastes a stroke, not once in a year. He plays each shot for everything it's worth."

There is a story about Player emptying a shagbag on the practice green and making one-foot putts for an entire hour. A fellow pro asked him what in the name of Harry Vardon he was doing. "I'm getting used to sinking putts," was Player's matter-of-fact answer.

There is no one quite like him. The interesting part of researching a profile of a famous person is that something about him almost always astonishes you because it doesn't fit with his public image or your private expectations. I have known Gary Player fairly well for almost 15 years now, and I never fail to be amazed at the way he will hear out and even solicit suggestions about his golf swing from lit-erally anybody: journalists, marshals, fans, milkmen.

It is not a common trait among great athletes. They don't exactly have closed minds or they wouldn't be great, but they tend like all of us to listen only to other experts or supposed experts in their specialized fields.

Player, I suspect, has a two-fold purpose in being so receptive to outside thinking, much of which is wholly frivolous. Not being able to see himself swing a club, he doesn't want to take the chance of ignoring somebody who has spotted something he hasn't considered, and he has the necessary facility to filter out meaningless information and experiment intelligently. And, being a visitor in other countries most of the time, he is reluctant to bruise anyone's sensitivities.

Even so, the extent of his open-mindedness is unique in sports as far as I can tell. California teaching professional Eddie Merrins talks about a case in point.

"He's going to learn from anybody he can," Merrins says. "I saw him at the 1973 Open at Oakmont. He'd read excerpts from my instruction book in *Golf Digest*, and was interested in my theories. I was in the parking lot at the Holiday Inn where I was staying, and he came running over and we had a little clinic right then and there. This was on Tuesday of U.S. Open week, when the last thing on most players' minds would be any thought of a swing change. Then I saw him on the practice range Friday. He was leading the U.S. Open — and he was out there hitting 600 balls, although he wasn't fully recovered

159

from major surgery, and he was working on something directly opposite of what he'd been working on earlier in the week!"

We see no indication that Player's awesome dedication is flagging. He reminds us when we compare all-time greats that a player really should not be evaluated until his career is done—and he implies that his is far from ended.

Paul Runyan, a respected teaching professional who twice won the PGA Championship, says, "Gary could be winning at a surprisingly advanced age. He's the only really well-conditioned athlete playing golf today, in my view. On a scale of 1 to 10, I'd rate him 9.6 or 9.7 in physical excellence. He works at it, every day. That's why he can travel so much and not suffer from it. I don't think he knows what jet lag is. Most of his physical excellence at the game is acquired, not God-given."

Player was jogging regularly 10 years ago, before it became a national fad. More accurately, he was running—at a good clip—several miles a day through parking lots and public parks at odd hours. There were those motorized passers-by, he remembers, who thought he was crazy.

"I didn't care and still don't," he says. "When I run I feel better, eat better, rest better. My stamina is greater. I'm stronger and, as a consequence, I hit the ball farther. All these considerations make me a better player. But I think the single most important thing that running does for me — and can do for any reasonably healthy golfer — is sharpen my reflexes. For some reason you never hear or read about reflexes in golf, but they're crucial. Golf is not a game for a sluggish person, and if you are just a little bit dull you are apt to hit a fraction of an inch behind the ball. You may not miss making a good shot by much, but that little difference can add strokes to your score. Reflexes are very, very important in golf, believe me."

Says Jimmy Demaret, a peer of Ben Hogan's, "Player is physically fit and self-disciplined, and I think he can be a super player for a few more years without exhausting himself. When he gets into his late 40's, his legs will get weak and then his nervous system will go. He won't be another Sam Snead, playing good golf at the age of 65. He isn't big enough. But in my time Player and Hogan are the most dedicated golfers I've ever seen, and I've seen a few."

When Gary Player disappears off the U.S. tour, he often heads for his 50-acre spread near Johannesburg, South Africa. The estate is called "Zonnehoeve," which means "a place in the sunshine." Pictured in front of the ranch house, above, are Gary and three of his six children: Wayne, Theresa and Jennifer. At right Gary checks out his prize horses with daughter Amanda.

Player for years has been golf's most devoted practicer of physical fitness. Here he works out with weights. Below, Gary observes closely as son Wayne, a scratch golfer, works on his game at the driving range on the property. Wayne hopes to be a professional golfer like his dad.

BOB TOSKI: Gary Player is a very intense little man, and his golf swing reflects his personality.

To start with, Player's position at address is too rigid for me. There's too much tension in his body. But that's the nature of the man. It's also his emulation of Ben Hogan. Hogan turned his arms out at address, but his arms were supple and relaxed. Gary turns his arms out like Hogan but tightens them up. His upper-body tension is too great. See how his shoulders are cramped together?

It all stems from what Gary thought Hogan was doing when he looked at him and studied pictures. A lot of folks misunderstood Hogan.

Further, Gary has a lot more flex in his knees and a lot more weight on his heels than most top players. That combination can only lead to a flat backswing with a tremendous amount of early rotation of the wrists, hands and club handle. His swing has to be inside-out.

And his weight at address is more on his left foot than his right foot, which I don't like to see in any player. It often creates the dreaded reverse weight shift — the weight

hangs left on the backswing and then falls back to the right on the downswing, when we want just the opposite.

Player does a lot of things well. At address his ball position is good, his grip position is good. But he has a very quick, tight backswing compared to most good players.

At the top of his swing, Gary's left wrist is a little cupped, but that doesn't hurt him as much as it might, because his clubface is square. He started his swing with a slightly cupped wrist. He has made a fine upper-body turn, even though he is hitting only a middle iron in this sequence. His back is facing the target, and he has swung his arms so that his left shoulder is under his chin.

His weight could be behind the ball more. He didn't really get off his left side on the backswing, and his swing plane was flat, so now he has to strain to shift his weight on the downswing. He starts down by pushing strongly with his right knee and right side, instead of pulling with his left knee and left arm as I would prefer. That's why he fights a hook. His bad shot goes

from left to left. His right hand gets too active on the downswing and closes the clubface in the hitting area.

Fortunately for Gary, his legs usually work very well through the ball, keeping his hands from taking over completely. His lower body is really moving. But his head sometimes goes with his lower body, and that costs him control.

The amazing thing about Player that I still don't understand is the position of his head as he moves back to the ball. His head rotates to his left and his eyes point to the

right of his target. Most good players' heads swivel backwards, if anything.

He loses his balance because his weight remained on his right leg too long and he hasn't shifted more weight to his left leg to support his downswing. He shifts his weight much better with a shorter club than with a longer one, as we see here with a 5-iron.

He has a marvelously straight left arm throughout his swing. Do you realize how much body antagonism and concentrated effort it takes for a person to do that? First

of all, the arm must be strong enough to sustain the momentum of the swing. You just don't keep your left arm straight in the golf swing unless you think about it, because there isn't anything you do in your lifestyle that tells you to keep your left arm straight. I'd rather see the average guy swing back with his left arm slightly bent, then straighten it coming down, than try to keep the left arm perfectly straight going back and bend it coming down. Player remarkably has the discipline and strength to keep the left arm firm throughout the swing, which gives his swing a solid radius.

In sum, Gary creates a lot of body·tension but can overcome that to some degree because he's so physically fit. He's an athlete and a superb one. The average handicap player trying to play golf Gary's way, not being an athlete and playing only once or twice a week, has no chance.

TOM WEISKOPF

When the co-founders of the DYCO Institute, a personality testing firm in Pennsylvania, approached *Golf Digest* magazine about putting together an article on the tour stars, I sensed that they were impelled by co-considerations. Like all smart businessmen, they wanted media exposure. And like all golfers and golf fans, they wanted to find out what makes Tom Weiskopf tick.

Weiskopf is closer to 40 than 30 now, and has won a dozen events and more than a million and a half dollars since he turned professional in 1964. But almost everyone — including Weiskopf himself — believes he has not really approached his potential. "With that swing," says another leading money winner, "he ought to win every time he tees it up."

It is generally agreed among his peers that Weiskopf has the best swing on the tour. Jack Nicklaus, who is not given to outbursts of enthusiasm about other players'

games, says, "He is just about as good as anybody ever has been at every point in the swing." If you were going to build the ideal composite golfer, from the ground up, it would be hard to improve on the rangy, well-proportioned Weiskopf.

Like Nicklaus, he gears his schedule each year to the four major championships, but through the 1977 season Weiskopf had won only one, the 1973 British Open. He frequently has been close in the Masters, where his dazzling ability to hit towering iron shots is particularly suited to the course. But no green jacket and no cigar.

Why hasn't Weiskopf lived up to our great expectations for him?

Quite obviously, his problem, such as it is, isn't physical, although he has quietly endured a bothersome hand injury for several years. He is the first to say so.

The problem, then, must be psychological. One pundit says Weiskopf has a one-piece swing and a two-piece personality. Weiskopf's friends—and he has many good ones, it surprises some people to hear—call him Big T, which could stand for Tom or for Talent . . . . or for Temperamental. We probably will remember Weiskopf as readily for his frequent peccadillos as for his great shots.

It has to be stressed that Weiskopf, whose mind is bright and searching, is at least as intrigued by his notorious personality as is everyone else. He willingly, enthusiastically submitted to the DYCO test, which consisted of picking words he felt most and least characterized him from among numerous sets of adjectives. Here is how the testing people evaluated him:

"Recently, after a particularly frustrating round in tournament play, Tom Weiskopf succumbed to his mercurial temper, packed his bags in mid-tournament and went home to Columbus without notifying his playing partners, the officials or the news media.

"Why would a professional of Weiskopf's great talent decide to violate the rules of golf and good sportsmanship in this manner? It would be easy to conclude that Tom has a swollen ego, doesn't care who he offends, and believes the tour needs him more than he needs the tour. These conclusions would make good logic, but they would be wrong. Tom is a supremely proud individual, but he can hate himself for having made an impulsive mistake, as you and I can.

"Tom's questionnaire shows us that despite his great talent he has mixed emotions about his occupation. Despite his skills and his achievements on the professional golf tour, he shows evidence of continually questioning the worth and significance of what he is doing. A naturally forceful and decisive person, he modifies all of his other behavioral characteristics to achieve a lifestyle quite different from his inner personality. By nature a confident, optimistic person, he has been steered by circumstances toward becoming suspicious of the motives of others while holding himself aloof.

"Inclined originally to be systematic and a seeker of consistent results, he has become a solution seeker looking for problems to solve. He is analyzing, investigating, tenaciously applying creative logic in a continuing quest for a clear-cut highway to the future.

"Tom Weiskopf is still searching for career objectives, and when things go wrong, as they invariably will on a golf course, he is more prone to explode mentally than a golfer of a less intense and complex nature. It is certain, however, that he will not realize his potential for top tournament play until he learns to accept the realities of life instead of continually questioning them.

"Possibly Tom can do too many things well. He should probably relax in the knowledge that his great talents are recognized and that in golf there is no such thing as perfection. He should accentuate his optimism and leave pessimism

His 1973 triumph in the British Open at Troon was one of an amazing five championships Weiskopf won in an eight-tournament stretch.

and suspicion for those less talented, while focusing his ability to concentrate and evaluate on just one shot at a time."

The DYCO analysis of Weiskopf would seem to help us understand one of his latest nonconforming moves, his rejection of a spot on the 1977 United States Ryder Cup team that played in Britain. To most pros, even the superstars, representing their country in the storied international series is a primary goal. They admit to getting goose bumps when the flags are raised and the bands play the national anthems. Not Weiskopf, however.

I was with him in the posh locker room at the Memorial Tournament in Ohio in the spring of the year when he divulged his intention not to play. Weiskopf was sitting at one of the card tables with a couple of other players, in a soft black leather chair, sipping iced tea and discussing his priorities. Joining them in the middle of the conversation, I assumed he was talking about golf. His subject was the grand slam, and he was saying how a man gets only so many chances at the four big ones and cannot afford to pass them by. As it turned out, he was talking about hunting bighorn sheep.

"Hunting is my great avocation, my emotional outlet," he said. "Bighorn are the premier animals to hunt. It's like a fisherman going for tarpon. There are four species of bighorn, and they constitute the grand slam of hunting. I've bagged two of the four, and I have a chance in the fall to get another, in Alberta, Canada. You have to make your plans more than a year in advance,

and I set this up long ago. If I don't go this fall, I may not have another chance for 10 years—maybe never. If you don't hunt, you can't understand what I'm saying, but this is more important to me than the Ryder Cup matches."

Weiskopf ordered another iced tea and his voice took on an icier tone as he talked about how he felt he was being persecuted, in effect, by the commissioner's office. (At that time he was still on a year's probation—he was also fined $3,000, though it never was announced—for walking off the course in the middle of the second round at the 1976 Westchester tournament. It was the fourth time that year that Weiskopf had made a premature exit, and it gave rise to a new phrase in the tour lexicon: When a player picked up before finishing a round, he henceforth was said to have "Weiskopfed it.") Weiskopf recently had been called onto the commissioner's carpet for what the player considered no good reason other than to remind him he was under continuous scrutiny, and he said it was hurting his play and diminishing his interest in the game.

He said Johnny Miller had picked up as many times as he had, but wasn't being harassed by the tour management. He said there always were reasons for his pullouts that never were aired. "I've made mistakes walking off golf courses," he said. "I don't like myself when I do those things, and I think I'm maturing to the point I won't do them again. I didn't want to say anything about it, but at Westchester I couldn't concentrate on my golf because one of my best friends, Bert Yancey, was having a nervous breakdown. He went from the tournament to the hospital for three months. I didn't tell anybody about it because it was nobody's business. I suffered more for Bert than for being fined and put on probation, but I just had to get away from there. If I had it to do over again, I would have played those six holes. I should have played them. But at the time I just couldn't do it."

An avid conversationalist, Weiskopf went on to generalize about his controversial temperament. "Only one person knows me, and that's me," he said. "I have never considered myself a bad guy or a prima donna. I'm a perfectionist. When you're called a superstar and don't turn out to be a superstar all the time, then the press sees you as temperamental. When I'm playing badly, I'm Terrible Tom. But when I'm playing well, I'm Terrific Tom.

"I'm not the character the press has portrayed. When things go wrong, I blame myself. I get mad at myself, not anybody else, and I say and do things I shouldn't. I'm emotional and easily upset, and bad shots get to me. They prey on my mind to the point I'm blind to others around me."

Some of his fellow pros think Weiskopf can be insufferably aloof when things are not going to his satisfaction. Snaps Dave Hill, the tour's most outspoken player: "He's had a hard time learning that winning golf is hard work and nobody gets all good breaks. He's spoiled and conceited and thinks everything should go exactly the way he wants it to. He reminds me of a kid I used to play marbles with. When he couldn't win he'd pick up his marbles and go home.

"I've never wanted to have anything to do with Weiskopf because he can go weeks without speaking to you. You can say hello in the locker room and he'll walk by you without a word. He did it to Bob Goalby one day and Goalby was going to break him in half.

"Weiskopf is very moody. I can sympathize with him there because I'm very moody, too. But his moodiness turns inward and mine comes out. Weiskopf broods where I just let it all hang out and then forget it. My way is healthier. When he is up, he is way up. But when he's down, he's morose. He has great desire and expects more of himself than he gets. He realizes how awesome his potential is and knows that he hasn't lived up to it often enough, and that has to be depressing to him.

"He has to reconcile himself to life going against him now and then—be more realistic. When he doesn't do well he has to act decently to people even if he doesn't feel like it. The sun does not rise and set for Tom Weiskopf alone."

The DYCO man who interpreted Weiskopf's personality test, reading between his own lines, wondered whether Weiskopf owed his outwardly dichotomous temperament to a spectacular early success when he first came on the tour—a high grade of performance that he could not consistently maintain.

In truth, Weiskopf's first four years as a pro were mostly disappointing. He made $89,407 and says you could not put a price on what he learned. But he didn't win, which was surprising in light of the expansive predictions of greatness for him. During his rookie year, Tony Lema said, "He's going to be a great one before you know it." Arnold Palmer, still the king then, called him the rookie most likely to succeed. Jack Nicklaus didn't see how Weiskopf could miss.

But Nicklaus and the rest of us failed to appreciate the strain that Weiskopf was under trying to become another Nicklaus. In 1966, Weiskopf lost 20 pounds and missed several tournaments due to a near-ulcerous stomach affliction brought on, probably, by the excessive demands others put on him and he put on himself.

A tall, handsome young man with an expressive face, Weiskopf was expected to be the next American golf hero. He was a big hitter out of Ohio State University like Nicklaus, and he immediately would start knocking off major titles the way Jack did when he joined the tour.

"Ohio State is a big sports school and you're going to get a lot of publicity," Weiskopf says in reflecting on those days. "Jack was a junior there when I was a freshman — neither one of us finished school — and I was always being compared to him. But the comparisons were unfair. People didn't realize that Jack had been playing seriously since he was about 10 but I learned most of my golf from Bob Kepler, the coach at Ohio State. I didn't start playing until I was 16 when Jack was already playing in the U.S. Amateur. As a kid I played baseball, basketball and football, but not golf. Then I began caddieing as a summer job and did that for two years. Watching the thrills and disappointments the game produced piqued my interest, and I decided it would be fun to play myself. Both of my parents played and were good golfers, but they didn't belong to a club. I would run down to the football field in our neighborhood and hit short irons till dark. In high school, I never won any tournaments. But I won the state Jaycee title and got a partial scholarship to Ohio State for baseball and golf. They even said I caddied for Jack at Ohio State, but I've never carried Jack's bag in my life, not even to help him pack it into a car. They said I would be another Nicklaus, and maybe I read those stories and believed them. Everybody has an ego, and you have to be awfully strong not to let that sort of thing affect you.

"When I turned pro, I hadn't had much experience in big amateur tournaments because I couldn't afford it, and I didn't have the patience and powers of concentration to win out there. For quite a while my distance off the tee worked against me. I didn't want to disappoint the fans who came out to see me drive the ball a mile, so I'd swing for the fence all the time. The Ohio State Scarlet Course, a great course, is over 7,200 yards long, which probably is why the school has turned out so many big hitters —Nicklaus, myself, Tom Nieporte, Dick Rhyan, Ed Sneed. I'd get on the tee on tour and hear some guy say 'There's the kid who hits it farther than Nicklaus' and I'd swing as hard as I could. My distance was usually terrific, but my direction left a lot to be desired.

"It took me a while to learn to watch my club selection with the irons under pressure, too. I'd get so pumped up I'd hit the ball 15 to 25 yards farther than normal. One year at Doral, I was near the lead in the third round and had a 155-yard shot to the 18th green. I knocked a 9-iron clear into the bleachers behind the green! At the Hope tournament I kept hitting way over the green on the par-3 holes. In most other sports you want to get all fired up, but in golf you have to be in control of your emotions at all times. It's really a difficult thing for an excitable guy like me. Disciplined imagination is the key to winning golf. By that I mean you have to consider all the possibilities for a shot and visualize it before you hit it. Ben Hogan was the best at imagining a shot, then turning over the actual execution to muscle memory. I've watched him every chance I've had—I just wish he were still on the tour so I could study him regularly."

Weiskopf smoothed out and firmed up his swing, to the point it could be a model for a good player, especially a tall one. Weiskopf is taller than any great player yet, 6'3", which evoked an interesting theory about his delayed development from Deane Beman, now the tour commissioner, when Weiskopf finally exploded during a six-week span in the spring of 1973 to win three tournaments, finish second and third (in the U.S. Open), and make more than $100,000. "The bigger you are, the farther you can hit

the ball and the easier the game will come to you," said Beman, who is barely bigger than a ball washer himself. "You tend to work less than a little fellow like me. The small man tries harder — of necessity. Tom was blessed with great natural ability and he never had to work that hard to make a good living. If you can do well with what you start with, why practice a lot? He never made the effort until this year, never put it together."

Weiskopf says the death of his father early in 1973 was the turning point in his career. "He was my most loyal fan," Tom says. "He made every sacrifice so I could become a good player. He gave up his vacations to save money for the best equipment. He always encouraged me. When he died, it woke me up. I took stock and realized I hadn't taken full advantage of my talent. I had let my father down, and I resolved to make up for that. I became determined to be a great player. I worked hard on my swing."

Weiskopf swings in excellent balance, with exceptionally repetitive tempo. "Probably the most important fundamental is good tempo," he says. "My definition of tempo is having complete control over the club from the moment your swing starts back, all the way into the follow-through. I've worked a lot on tempo with Tommy Bolt, who has probably the greatest tempo I've ever seen. Early in my career I swung too fast under pressure. I'd take the club too far past parallel at the top and lose control. The main thing Tommy told me was that if you have a slow tempo, which I

basically do, you always should swing slowly. If you have a fast tempo, as Arnold Palmer does, then you always should swing fast. In other words, don't be erratic with your tempo — practice making it consistent.

"The thing that usually destroys tempo," Weiskopf continues, "is too much speed at the start of the swing. Once you snatch the club away from the ball with the right hand, you've lost control, and if you don't have control of the club you'll never be firm at the top. When Bolt gets to the top of his swing, even today, he's in such great control of the club you think you could run up to him and do chin-ups on it.

"I find one of the best ways to maintain consistent tempo is with the waggle and preshot routine. I waggle the club the same way for each shot, never varying it. And I start each shot on the same count. I put the club down, look twice and then go. If you made me go a fraction of a second early or late, it would completely destroy my tempo and the timing of the swing."

Weiskopf's full swing makes him, in the opinion of most of his rivals, the best driver of his generation, even better than Nicklaus, and the preeminent long-iron player. Says Frank Beard, "Nicklaus is a tremendously strong, accurate, pressure-proof driver, but if I had to bet on one of those two big Buckeyes to slam it into the fairway, I'd bet on Weiskopf. He seems to be more confident about his big swing—I wonder at times if Jack is dead sure he'll put the ball on a dime 295 yards up the fairway. Weiskopf is that sure of himself off the tee." Not even Nicklaus propels the ball with the long irons as high as Weiskopf, who swings a 2-iron almost effortlessly; he literally swings the 2-iron at the same pace he swings an 8-iron.

Weiskopf's awesome long game tends to obscure a well-rounded short game. "He has," in the estimation of one expert, "a wider variety of shots than anybody else playing today." His putting ranges from good to sensational.

The public also does not appreciate that Weiskopf is respected by many of the younger tour pros for his teaching ability. Jerry Pate, for example, says Weiskopf's coaching helped him win the U.S. Open in 1976.

Says good friend Frank Beard, "He works with a lot of us. He's very generous with his time and advice. He'll help anybody who asks him. There's a lot more to Tom Weiskopf than you might think, a lot of sides that the galleries don't see. He enjoys people, but I often sense that fans come out to watch him for the same reason many people go to auto races: They want to see a wreck, see some gory excitement. They come to see if Tom will throw a club or stalk off the course. Consequently, the Tom Weiskopf I see on the golf course now is not the Tom Weiskopf I know and enjoy as a stimulating dinner companion.

"It's as if he's looking over his shoulder all the time, afraid of some specter hiding somewhere waiting for him to make a slip, to use profanity, to say something that could be misprinted in the paper—something he could be criticized for. He can't be the Tom Weiskopf he wants to be. This creates a vicious circle. By keeping his emotions penned up he puts additional pressure on himself, and when he finally gets to the point he can't stand it anymore, he explodes again.

"I think the fans might be more sympathetic—and not as quick to pass judgment on his foibles — if they could know Tom Weiskopf the way some of us know him privately. I've heard it said that he's not very smart, and maybe this stems from his occasional displays of bad judgment on the course. Well, he's far from stupid. He's an extremely intelligent man who can talk to you on almost any subject. He's a relaxed person to be with. He never wants to argue or fight with you.

"I wish Tom himself could see what a different person he is in private than in public. Because the sad fact is that his troubles and the pressures boiling inside him—self-inflicted or imposed by others — have kept him from achieving all the success that his physical skills could bring him. There is no doubt in my mind that he still could reach unbelievable heights, but whether he does depends on how he resolves this ongoing feud with himself. If Tom can just relax and realize that a lot of people would really like to pull for him, would love to be friendly and see him play well, then I think he could achieve greater things.

"Otherwise, I'm afraid Tom might consider an early retirement from golf. He's obviously close to having all the money he'll ever need. An early departure by Weiskopf would be too bad, because the game would lose a great player and, in my opinion, a great guy."

Another aspect of Weiskopf's many-sided personality that is seldom on display is his engaging sense of humor, most evident in a regaling knack for story-telling. He can reduce his companions to tears of laughter with his Tommy Bolt temper stories, and I still remember with a chuckle the story he told about himself during the British Open at Carnoustie in 1975.

He was staying at the Old Course Hotel in St. Andrews, 20 minutes across the bay from Carnoustie by hovercraft for the adventurous. The beauty of summer golf in Scotland is that there is enough daylight to tee off at 6:30 in the evening and get in a full round before dinner. That's what Weiskopf and three American friends, non-competitors in the Open, set out to do early in the week at St. Andrews' storied Old Course.

Weiskopf introduced himself at the starter's hut near the first tee, expecting the glorifying treatment to which tour stars are accustomed, like free green fees and a starting time immediately if not sooner.

"That'll be two pounds and you'll follow those folks over there," snapped the venerable starter in a burr you could cut with a sand wedge, pointing at a gaggle of locals on a park bench.

"Do British Open champions have to pay?" asked Weiskopf, more bemused than offended.

"Aye," said the starter. "This is a public course. Two pounds each."

Upon payment, Weiskopf was handed a plain little scorecard.

"I'd like three more scorecards," he said. "We're going to have a lot of bets to keep track of."

"One card to a group," said the starter, crisply.

Weiskopf waited his turn to tee off and then — when the starter called "Play away!"—went as far back on the tee as he could go, as pros will do. The starter popped out of the shed and admonished Weiskopf to tee off up between the single set of boxes, the same as everyone else.

Known for his Vesuvian temper, Weiskopf could only collapse with laughter at this final comeuppance. He had to pay like everyone else, he had to settle for only one scorecard for his group, and he had to play from the short tees.

Recalling the incident, he marvels, "That's St. Andrews."

That's also, believe it or not, Tom Weiskopf.

"I've put too much pressure on myself in the past," he says pensively. "I could be playing well and still not enjoy myself on the course. I was too tight. I never laughed at anything. Now I want to have a good time out there. Golf isn't the only thing in the world. My attitude changed for the better when I got married and it changed even more when we had kids."

The questions rage on. How good could Tom Weiskopf be, with all that talent, if he didn't have that temperament? If he didn't, of course, he wouldn't be Tom Weiskopf, he would be somebody else.

He says with a grin, "I've always been great copy, haven't I?"

178

Tom Weiskopf relishes the challenge of hunting almost as much as the challenge of golf. Above, a bearded Weiskopf and friend pose with a bighorn sheep bagged in Alberta, Canada. At right, a pleased Tom with a quarry nailed in Kenya, Africa. Weiskopf even passed up a berth on the U.S. Ryder Cup team in 1977 to pursue Canadian bighorn sheep.

The other Weiskopfs: wife Jeanne, a former Miss Minnesota, and children Eric and Heidi. Below, Tom on another hunting expedition in northern Canada, a haven from the pressures of tournament golf.

BOB TOSKI: It's hard to overesti-mate the importance of a good set-up. More than anything else, your address position and posture deter-mine how you will swing the club. Tom Weiskopf's setup is probably the finest in golf — and his swing may be the best in the game.

I personally think Tom is as good a golfer as Jack Nicklaus, although his record doesn't compare. Tom's mechanics are about as good as Jack's, but Tom doesn't concentrate and get the ball in the hole as well as Jack does. Nobody does.

I couldn't collaborate with an artist and draw a better setup than

Tom's: The ball is forward in his stance, most of his weight is on the inside of his right foot, his head is behind the ball about on a line with his right knee, his knees are slightly flexed with his weight toward the balls of his feet, and he is bent from the hips with his back straight and his arms hanging freely. His arms and legs are alive and primed to go.

From such a sound setup posi-tion, Tom almost has to make a good swing. He has done every-thing he can to preview his impact position before he ever starts to swing. He has simplified his weight

shift by positioning his upper body behind the ball with most of his weight on his right side. He doesn't have to work to get behind the ball at the top of his swing — he's already back there.

Waist high on his backswing, he is maintaining an excellent extension of the left arm and getting a good stretching appearance along the back of his left hand, arm and shoulder. That extension creates a big, wide swing arc and stores up power for release on the downswing. With the left arm straight here, it will tend to be straight later.

Notice how Weiskopf's left heel

stays close to the ground as he approaches the top of his swing. The bigger, stronger player can keep his left heel down and still have enough flexibility to get behind the ball and make a strong move back down, but the smaller, less supple player restricts himself too much. In most swings, I prefer to see the left heel coming up some.

The marvelous feature of Weiskopf's backswing is the way he swings his arms smoothly up and around his right side, with the shoulders following. The pace of his arm swing is exquisite. He sets the club in position at the top quiet-

183

ly, with no forced effort. Too many players lose sight of the purpose of the backswing, which is simply to *set the club in position for the downswing.*

About the only thing I don't like about Tom's swing is his clubface position at the top — it's a little closed. He bows his left wrist near the top of the swing and shuts the face. If he were to work his left forearm more upward, the hand would not "lay off" like that.

Weiskopf starts the downswing with his legs, driving his knees laterally. The left knee is pulling and the right knee is pushing, and his

upper body is "quiet"—especially the right hand, which remains passive at the start of the downswing. The arms and hands soon are pulled down by the forward thrust of the lower body, and they swing freely in response to the action of the legs.

Halfway down, Weiskopf has not yet released the angle between his left forearm and the shaft of the club—the angle he set on the backswing. Remember that left-arm extension he established then? Well, retaining that extension now enables him to delay the release of the angle so he can get maximum club-

head speed.

At impact, Weiskopf is fantastically good. His head has hardly moved since he started his swing. His left heel is back where it started. His left arm is firm and extended, and his legs are driving.

Let me make a point here about the action of the right knee that could help many average players. A lot of people don't realize how crucial it is to keep the right knee moving toward the left knee on the downswing—to keep the right knee chasing the left knee. Too many weekend players hang back on the right leg on the downswing and

don't get their weight shifted into the shot. Weiskopf's right knee is catching up to his left as he comes into the ball.

Swinging into his follow-through, his head stays back but his arms extend through the shot. His head is beginning to rotate around to his left, but he is in no hurry to look up and follow the flight of the ball.

His follow-through shows him in perfect balance. He is relaxed, which means he has exerted no undue effort during his swing. It is the outstanding conclusion to an outstanding swing.

CAREER RECORDS

MAJOR VICTORIES (2)   **RAY FLOYD**

1969   PGA Championship
1976   Masters

TOUR VICTORIES (10)

1963   St. Petersburg Open
1965   St. Paul Open
1969   Greater Jacksonville Open, American Golf Classic,
       PGA Championship
1975   Kemper Open
1976   Masters, World Open
1977   Byron Nelson Golf Classic, Pleasant Valley Classic

CAREER EARNINGS

$1,039,167 (through 1977)

OTHER ACHIEVEMENTS

National Jaycee Champion—1960. Ryder Cup teams—1969, 1975,
1977.

MAJOR VICTORY   **AL GEIBERGER**

1966   PGA Championship

TOUR VICTORIES (11)

1962   Caracas Open, Ontario Open
1963   Almaden Open
1965   American Golf Classic
1966   PGA Championship
1974   Sahara Invitational
1975   Tournament of Champions, Tournament Players Championship
1976   Greater Greensboro Open, Western Open
1977   Danny Thomas Memphis Classic

CAREER EARNINGS

$1,077,972 (through 1977)

OTHER ACHIEVEMENTS

National Jaycee Champion—1954. Ryder Cup teams—1967, 1975.

MAJOR VICTORY

HALE IRWIN

1974   U.S. Open

TOUR VICTORIES (10)

1971   Sea Pines Heritage Classic
1973   Sea Pines Heritage Classic
1974   U.S. Open
1975   Western Open, Atlanta Golf Classic
1976   Glen Campbell Los Angeles Open, Florida Citrus Open
1977   Atlanta Classic, Colgate Hall of Fame Classic,
         San Antonio-Texas Open

CAREER EARNINGS

$1,234,230 (through 1977)

OTHER ACHIEVEMENTS

NCAA Champion—1967. Piccadilly World Match Play
Champion—1974, 1975. Ryder Cup team—1975, 1977.

MAJOR VICTORIES (2)

JOHNNY MILLER

1973   U.S. Open
1976   British Open

TOUR VICTORIES (17)

1971   Southern Open
1972   Sea Pines Heritage Classic
1973   U.S. Open
1974   Bing Crosby National Pro-Am, Phoenix Open, Dean Martin
         Tucson Open, Sea Pines Heritage Classic, Tournament of
         Champions, Westchester Classic, World Open, Kaiser
         International Open
1975   Phoenix Open, Dean Martin Tucson Open, Bob Hope Desert
         Classic, Kaiser International Open
1976   NBC Tucson Open, Bob Hope Desert Classic

CAREER EARNINGS

$1,144,065 (through 1977)

OTHER ACHIEVEMENTS

Junior Amateur Champion—1964. Winning World Cup individual and
team (with Nicklaus) champion—1973, 1975. Byron Nelson Award—
1974. Ryder Cup team—1975. PGA Player of the Year—1974.

MAJOR VICTORIES (16)

1959 U.S. Amateur
1961 U.S. Amateur
1962 U.S. Open
1963 Masters, PGA Championship
1965 Masters
1966 Masters, British Open
1967 U.S. Open
1970 British Open
1971 PGA Championship
1972 Masters, U.S. Open
1973 PGA Championship
1975 Masters, PGA Championship

TOUR VICTORIES (63)

1962 U.S. Open, Seattle World's Fair Open, Portland Open
1963 Palm Springs Golf Classic, Masters, Tournament of Champions, PGA Championship, Sahara Invitational
1964 Portland Open, Tournament of Champions, Phoenix Open, Whitemarsh Open
1965 Portland Open, Masters, Memphis Classic, Thunderbird Classic, Philadelphia Golf Classic
1966 Masters, Sahara Invitational, PGA National Team Championship (with Palmer)
1967 U.S. Open, Sahara Invitational, Bing Crosby National Pro-Am, Western Open, Westchester Classic
1968 Western Open, American Golf Classic
1969 Sahara Invitational, Kaiser International Open, Andy Williams San Diego Open
1970 Byron Nelson Golf Classic, National Four-Ball Championship (with Palmer)
1971 PGA Championship, Tournament of Champions, Byron Nelson Golf Classic, National Team Championship (with Palmer), Walt Disney World Open
1972 Bing Crosby National Pro-Am, Doral-Eastern Open, Masters, U.S. Open, Westchester Classic, U.S. Professional Match Play, Walt Disney World Open
1973 Bing Crosby National Pro-Am, Greater New Orleans Open, Tournament of Champions, Atlanta Golf Classic, PGA Championship, Ohio Kings Island Open, Walt Disney World Golf Classic
1974 Hawaiian Open, Tournament Players Championship
1975 Doral-Eastern Open, Sea Pines Heritage Classic, Masters, PGA Championship, World Open

1976 Tournament Players Championship, World Series of Golf
1977 Jackie Gleason Inverrary Classic, Tournament of Champions,
      Memorial Tournament

CAREER EARNINGS

$3,092,720 (through 1977)

OTHER ACHIEVEMENTS

NCAA Champion—1961. Winning World Cup teams—1963, 1964,
1966, 1967, 1971, 1973. Byron Nelson Award—1964, 1965, 1967,
1972, 1973, 1975. Australian Open Champion—1964, 1968, 1971,
1975, 1976. Ryder Cup teams—1969, 1971, 1973, 1975, 1977.
PGA Player of the Year—1967, 1972, 1973, 1975, 1976.

MAJOR VICTORIES (8)   ARNOLD PALMER

1954 U.S. Amateur
1958 Masters
1960 Masters, U.S. Open
1961 British Open
1962 Masters, British Open
1964 Masters

TOUR VICTORIES (61)

1955 Canadian Open
1956 Insurance City Open, Eastern Open, Panama Open*,
      Colombian Open*
1957 Houston Open, Azalea Open, Rubber City Open,
      San Diego Open
1958 St. Petersburg Open, Masters, Pepsi Championship
1959 Thunderbird Invitational, Oklahoma City Open,
      West Palm Beach Open
1960 Insurance City Open, Masters, Palm Springs Golf Classic,
      Texas Open, Baton Rouge Open, Pensacola Open, U.S. Open,
      Mobile Sertoma Open
1961 San Diego Open, Texas Open, Baton Rouge Open,
      Phoenix Open, Western Open
1962 Masters, Palm Springs Golf Classic, Texas Open, Phoenix Open,
      Tournament of Champions, Colonial National Invitational,
      American Golf Classic
1963 Thunderbird Classic, Pensacola Open, Phoenix Open,
      Western Open, Los Angeles Open, Cleveland Open,
      Whitemarsh Open

      * Not counted as an official PGA Tour event.

(Palmer cont.)
1964   Oklahoma City Open, Masters
1965   Tournament of Champions
1966   Los Angeles Open, Tournament of Champions, Houston
       Champions International, PGA National Team Championship
       (with Nicklaus)
1967   Los Angeles Open, Tucson Open, American Golf Classic,
       Thunderbird Classic
1968   Bob Hope Desert Classic, Kemper Open
1969   Heritage Golf Classic, Danny Thomas Diplomat Classic
1970   National Four-Ball Championship (with Nicklaus)
1971   Bob Hope Desert Classic, Florida Citrus Invitational, Westchester
       Classic, National Team Championship (with Nicklaus)
1973   Bob Hope Desert Classic

CAREER EARNINGS

$1,762,081 (through 1977)

OTHER ACHIEVEMENTS

Winning World Cup teams—1960, 1962, 1963, 1964, 1965,
1966, 1967. Ryder Cup teams—1961, 1965, 1967, 1971, 1973. Byron
Nelson Award—1957, 1960, 1961, 1962, 1963. Australian Open—
1966. Spanish Open—1975. British PGA—1975. Vardon Trophy for
low stroke average—1961, 1962, 1964, 1967. PGA Player of the
Year—1960, 1962.

MAJOR VICTORIES (8)   **GARY PLAYER**

1959   British Open
1961   Masters
1962   PGA Championship
1965   U.S. Open
1968   British Open
1972   PGA Championship
1974   Masters, British Open

TOUR VICTORIES (18)

1958   Kentucky Derby Open
1961   Lucky International Open, Sunshine Open, Masters
1962   PGA Championship
1963   San Diego Open
1964   "500" Festival Open, Pensacola Open
1965   U.S. Open
1969   Tournament of Champions
1970   Greater Greensboro Open

1971   Greater Jacksonville Open, National Airlines Open
1972   Greater New Orleans Open, PGA Championship
1973   Southern Open
1974   Masters, Danny Thomas Memphis Classic

CAREER EARNINGS

$1,329,306 (through 1977)

OTHER ACHIEVEMENTS

South African Open—1956, 1960, 1965, 1966, 1967, 1968, 1969, 1972, 1975, 1976, 1977. Australian Open—1958, 1962, 1963, 1965, 1969, 1970, 1974. Piccadilly World Match Play Champion—1965, 1966, 1968, 1971, 1973. World Cup individual and team winner—1965, individual winner—1977. Brazilian Open—1972, 1974. Victories around the world—107.

MAJOR VICTORIES (5)   **LEE TREVINO**

1968   U.S. Open
1971   U.S. Open, British Open
1972   British Open
1974   PGA Championship

TOUR VICTORIES (20)

1968   U.S. Open, Hawaiian Open
1969   Tucson Open
1970   Tucson Open, National Airlines Open
1971   Tallahassee Open, Danny Thomas Memphis Classic, U.S. Open, Canadian Open, Sahara Invitational
1972   Danny Thomas Memphis Classic, Greater Hartford Open, Greater St. Louis Golf Classic
1973   Jackie Gleason Inverrary Classic, National Airlines Classic, Doral-Eastern Open
1974   Greater New Orleans Open, PGA Championship
1975   Florida Citrus Open
1976   Colonial National Invitational
1977   Canadian Open

CAREER EARNINGS

$1,620,723 (through 1977,

OTHER ACHIEVEMENTS

Ryder Cup teams—1969, 1971, 1973, 1975. Winning World Cup teams—1969, 1971. Byron Nelson Award—1971. Mexican Open—1975. Vardon Trophy winner for low stroke average—1970, 1971, 1972, 1974. PGA Player of the Year—1971.

MAJOR VICTORIES (3)   **TOM WATSON**

1975 British Open
1977 Masters, British Open

TOUR VICTORIES (6)

1974 Western Open
1975 Byron Nelson Golf Classic
1977 Bing Crosby National Pro-Am, Andy Williams San Diego Open,
      Masters, Western Open

CAREER EARNINGS

$838,962 (through 1977)

OTHER ACHIEVEMENTS

Ryder Cup team—1977. Byron Nelson Award—1977. Vardon
Trophy winner—1977. PGA Player of the Year—1977.

MAJOR VICTORY (1)   **TOM WEISKOPF**

1973 British Open

TOUR VICTORIES (12)

1968 Andy Williams San Diego Open, Buick Open
1971 Kemper Open, IVB-Philadelphia Golf Classic
1972 Jackie Gleason Inverrary Classic
1973 Colonial National Invitational, Kemper Open, IVB-Philadelphia
      Golf Classic, Canadian Open
1975 Greater Greensboro Open, Canadian Open
1977 Kemper Open

CAREER EARNINGS

$1,553,825 (through 1977)

OTHER ACHIEVEMENTS

Western Amateur Champion—1963. Piccadilly World Match
Play Champion—1972. Ryder Cup team—1973, 1975.